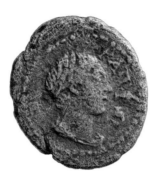

A LITTLE GAY HISTORY

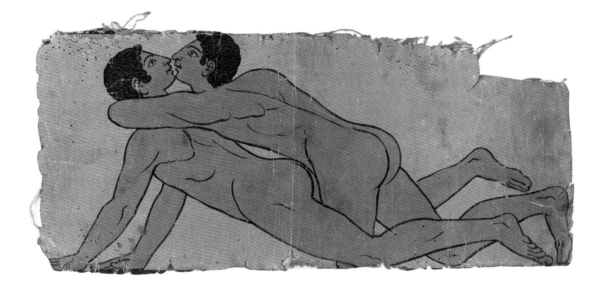

A LITTLE GAY HISTORY

DESIRE AND
DIVERSITY
ACROSS
THE WORLD

R. B. PARKINSON

WITH CONTRIBUTIONS BY

KATE SMITH AND MAX CAROCCI

Columbia University Press
New York

Columbia University Press
Publishers Since 1893
New York   Chichester, West Sussex
cup.columbia.edu
Copyright © 2013 The Trustees of the British Museum
All rights reserved

First published in 2013 by The British Museum Press
A division of The British Museum Company Ltd
The British Museum
Great Russell Street, London WC1B 3DG
britishmuseum.org/publishing

Library of Congress Cataloging-in-Publication Data
Parkinson, Richard B.
    A little gay history : desire and diversity across the world / Richard B. Parkinson
                p. cm.
    Includes bibliographical references.
    ISBN 978-0-231-16663-8 (pbk. : alk. paper)

Library of Congress Subject Data and Holding Information can be found on the
Library of Congress Online Catalog.
LCCN: 2013930735

∞

Columbia University Press books are printed on permanent and durable acid-free paper.
This book is printed on paper with recycled content.
Printed in Belgium by Graphius.

Front cover: Bust of the emperor Hadrian wearing military dress, Tivoli, c. AD 125–130.
Marble, H. 84 cm; Portrait head from a statue of Antinous wearing a wreath of ivy,
Rome, c. AD 130–140. Marble, H. 81 cm (© Trustees of the British Museum)

Back cover: Deck of playing cards depicting drag queens by Ōtsuka Takashi, Japan, 1997.
Paper, 10.5 x 7.2 cm (© Taq Ōtsuka)

Frontispiece: An Etruscan painting of two men, as copied in a nineteenth-century drawing of the
fifth-century BC 'Tomb of the Chariots', in a cemetery at Tarquinia, Italy.
Paper, 12.5 x 28.1 cm (© Trustees of the British Museum)

FSC
www.fsc.org
MIX
Paper | Supporting
responsible forestry
FSC® C014767

CONTENTS

PREFACE

Maurice, shall we re-write history?

E. M. Forster

This little book goes back a long way. It has grown out of a web-trail created by Kate Smith in 2007, which was later revised as a British Museum thematic web-trail produced by David Prudames and curated by R. B. Parkinson. This trail was launched as part of LGBT (lesbian, gay, bisexual and transgender) History Month in 2009, and a paper version was issued by Kate Smith in 2010 for Untold London (a Museum of London project). The success of these trails encouraged us to expand them into a book that would be a short accessible history for audiences regardless of age, gender or sexual identity. This book does not, of course, intend to be a political tract but only to raise awareness of the history of some often overlooked aspects of the human condition.

We want to show the depth of lesbian, gay, bisexual and transgender history and its presence in every continent across the world: 'homosexuality' is not just the well-known 'Greek love' of ancient Athens. So we have tried to explore as full a range of cultures and periods as we could from the British Museum's collection, while also including some of the well-known figures who have become iconic to 'gay' history. Desire and identity are not limited to sexual activity, but inevitably depictions of sex are the most unambiguous historical records that we have of such desire, and so a few of the images are quite explicit. This history has been compiled from the collection of a single museum with some additional material from our sister institution, the British Library, originally part of the British Museum. I am grateful to many other institutions for assistance and support, including the legendary Merchant Ivory Productions, IHLIA in Amsterdam and the Hall-Carpenter Archives in London. This book includes material from the earlier versions of the project; like any history, it is unavoidably partial and has many gaps, and the choice of objects and emphases is in part a personal one. The nature of identity politics and academia is such that, to quote the title of one of Bhupen Khakhar's paintings, *You Can't Please All*, and I can only apologize to any groups among the diverse lesbian, gay, bisexual and transgender communities who feel under-represented in this brief survey.

Much of the book has been researched by Kate Smith of Untold London, who has provided continuous inspiration and support for the project. Max Carocci has advised on some of the more modern objects from an anthropological perspective.

I am grateful to many colleagues, both in the British Museum and elsewhere, who have taken time from their schedules and helped me with areas of expertise very distant from my own: Philip Attwood; Steve Aucott; Richard Blurton; Lissant Bolton; Dirk Booms; Rosemary Bradley; Hugo Chapman; Kate Charlesworth; Tim Clark; Jill Cook; Sean Curran; Sona Datta; David Deitcher; Sue Donnelly; Thomas Dowson; Barbara Ewing; Stuart Frost; Amanda Gregory; Yannick Guillou; Achmy Halley; Julie Hudson; James Ivory; Ian Jenkins; Ivor Kerslake; Joachim and Angelika Konietzny; Jimmy MacSweeney; Lin McDevitt-Pugh; Colin McEwan; Margaret Maitland; Marcel Marée; Laurence Marsh; Robert Mills; Rictor Norton; Laura Philips; Jan Pimblett; Tim Reid; Paul Roberts; Seth Rubin; Judy Rudoe; Axelle Russo; Nigel Saint; Dan Selden; Kim Sloan; Bart Smith; Jan Stuart; Sian Toogood; Lonneke van den Hoonaard; Tania Watkins; Patricia Wheatley; Alice White. On a personal note, I have been touched by the support for this project across the Museum. Though I speak on behalf of many, responsibility for the tone of the whole remains entirely mine, and I apologize for anything that readers may find distracting, offensive or erroneous.

The book is dedicated to Gwendolen Reid-Parkinson, a much-missed family member, and to my partner/husband/whatever-I-am-allowed-to-call-him, Tim, *hospes comesque*.

R. B. P.

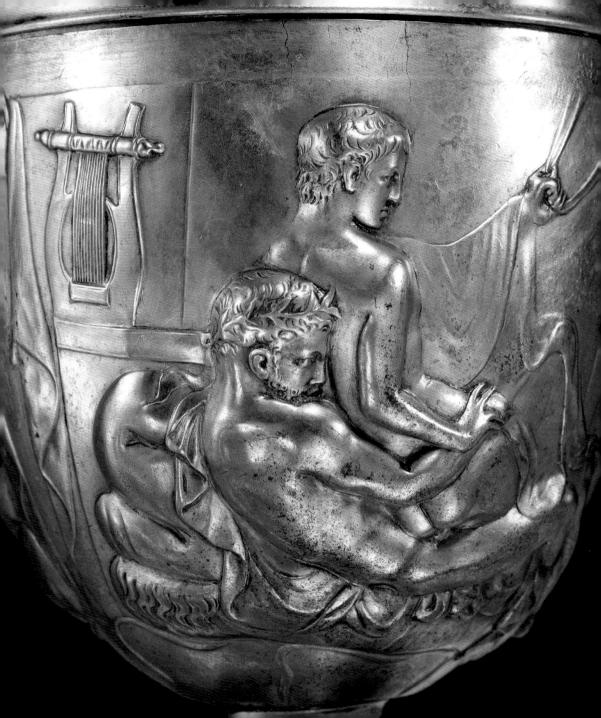

INTRODUCTION: 'A GREAT UNRECORDED HISTORY'

Please do not make me use the word homosexual, which I think too dangerous (for it enhances prejudices) and absurd. Say 'Gay' if you like, but it would be too recent a word to be used in this passage.

Marguerite Yourcenar, 1987

WORDS AND LABELS

It was quite hard to choose the title of this small book, but then words and identities are almost always difficult things. In the end, we went with 'gay', although it is a very modern term for identifying a person, and it is often taken to refer to men, rather than to both men and women. It is, however, a convenient and widely understood shorthand, like most of our terms for living, and the alternative labels seemed more problematic. 'Queer' is a reclaimed term of abuse which might sound too politically charged for some readers. 'Homosexual' is a term coined in the nineteenth century as part of the medicalization of human sexuality, and it can sound as if it is reducing people to scientific curiosities. These difficulties about the seemingly simple matter of a book's title hint at the different cultural values that have been placed on the apparently universal phenomenon that this book explores: people who tend to desire and love other people of the same sex.

The long stretch of world history increases the complexity. The Roman emperor Hadrian (AD 76–138) was not 'gay' in the modern senses of the word, but from what we know of his loves

Two Roman lovers, a detail from the 'Warren Cup'. Palestine, c. AD 10.

Silver, H. (bowl of cup) 8.3 cm.

it seems certain that he would have been 'gay' or 'bisexual' if he had lived in modern Europe. So we avoid using the word 'gay' for ancient societies, and refer to 'same-sex desire' which has fewer exclusively modern overtones. But this raises the question: is what we now term 'homosexuality' a modern concept or is it something that has always existed in different forms and names? Same-sex desire certainly seems to have been part of human experience from the earliest recorded times. In a poem from ancient Egypt, around 1800 BC, one male god tries to seduce another by saying 'What a lovely backside you have!' This is perhaps the earliest known chat-up line in human history, and it is between two men. So same-sex desire is not a recent invention, and evidence from so many cultures shows that it has not been 'imported' from one culture to others, as some people have claimed. But still the question remains: has such desire always been something that defines a person's identity, as it often has in the modern period?

Desire leaves no archaeological traces. 'Love' is always hard to pin down. It is sometimes difficult to fix precise boundaries to these feelings in our own lives, so it is not surprising that it is even harder with individuals from four thousand years ago. And such problems are not specific to *ancient* history. Trying to sense how similar and how different the past is to us is a fundamental part of the historical exercise. As David Halperin has noted, studying sexuality raises fundamental questions about identity and difference in writing history. The aim of this short book is not to outline any single answer to these complex questions, or to assert that certain attitudes are right or wrong. It is simply to present a few historical facts as we see them, and to remind all readers (regardless of their own desires) that love has always been diverse throughout history and across cultures. History has all too often been a list of the deeds of famous men who are implicitly 'heterosexual' and usually European. This approach has been very limiting, not least to women. Likewise, 'love' and 'romance' in many cultures are often portrayed as 'heterosexual' by default. This is also limiting, and can be dull for readers and viewers, unless they happen to belong to that category. Unsurprisingly, lesbian, gay, bisexual and transgender people have often felt excluded and silenced, and without a history. But this is simply not so: no one from these communities should feel alone in the world. As E. M. Forster noted 'there always have been people like me and there always will be'. So a more inclusive and interesting history of the world is possible, and same-sex desire does have a history – and in many forms.

FORMED BY CULTURE

How then do we find this love in the historical record? The difficulties seem immense. What different societies consider to be 'abnormal' or 'normal' has varied widely. Many types of sexual relations can go against the concerns for property and breeding that underlie the social norms in many (if not all) cultures, and so sex often runs the risk of disapproval and censure. In particular, some religions have regarded same-sex sexual activity as immoral, because it is thought to be against procreation and therefore 'unnatural'. Human societies have frequently been built around factors such as power, wealth and inheritance, and have often produced simple distinctions to categorize and control their members' desires.

Looking at a range of societies across time makes it clear that the realities of existence are actually more complex and contingent than this when it comes to both gender and desire. Many societies have created distinct and exclusive roles for men and women. The two genders often have supposedly inherent characteristics, as can be seen in ancient Egyptian art where men and women were given different skin tones as well as different physiques. But such fixed definitions are not invariably the case. In many cultures the gods often have both male and female attributes, raising the possibility that people also need not be viewed as rigidly male or female. Many cultures have articulated the existence of intermediate sexes, 'third' sexes and 'hermaphrodites', combining both sexes in one. Gender, like desire, is diverse and has been shaped and constructed in many different ways.

Even what is thought of as erotic or sexual can vary from culture to culture. In this sense, any male erection is a cultural creation: the same depiction can be, at various times and places, either a state-sanctioned piece of religious iconography or a bit of pornography for private viewing (see pp. 42–3). Carvings on some street corners in Roman cities, for example, show erections or even whole animals made up of erect phalluses (a 'phallus' is simply an academic penis). An erection was often a magical symbol or talisman against the evil eye in Mediterranean cultures, and these carvings are almost certainly protective devices to ward off evil from the building or road (opposite). But modern visitors often mis-read these inscriptions as signs for brothels, advertising sex for sale. Roman culture is comparatively recent, familiar and well documented; such embarrassing mistakes are even easier to make when thinking about more distant cultures. And when the evidence comes from wordless objects and is purely visual, it can be particularly hard to interpret. In Sicily, there are very early rock engravings from around 10,000 BC in the Grotta dell'Addaura which show two naked men lying close together, as part of a larger scene. Some historians have suggested that they show man on man sexual activity; if so, this would be the earliest known representation.

A carving of a phallic animal at a street corner in the Roman city of Leptis Magna in modern Libya, from around AD 200.

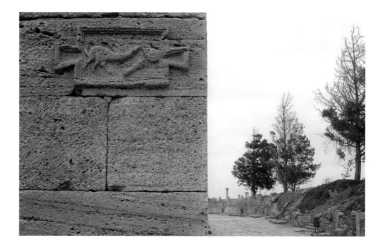

However, this is disputed by specialists, and other possible interpretations include acrobats, initiation ceremonies or (perhaps the most likely) ritual killings. It is impossible to have an infallible instinctive 'gaydar' across other cultures and periods, and the historian of desire has to proceed with some caution.

Close intimate relationships between two men or two women are not always sexual: they can be 'homosocial' rather than 'homosexual'. When two men kiss in some cultures, this can suggest a sexual aspect to their relationship, but this would not be the case in other cultures. And this uncertainty is nothing new. Homer's epic poem the *Iliad*, from around the eighth century BC, has at its centre the passionate relationship between the Greek warrior heroes Patroclus and Achilles. Different interpretations of the exact nature of this relationship existed among readers even in ancient times. The dividing line between friendship and love can be notoriously unstable. This has also been the case with some historical friendships between women, including – from a very different period – the married

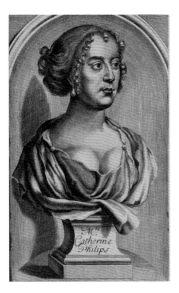

A portrait of the English poet Katherine Philips as a classical bust, after an engraving by William Faithorne. This was used to illustrate the 1667 edition of her poems. London, 1667.

Paper, 17 x 10 cm.

Englishwoman Katherine Philips (1631–64) (left). She wrote verse in praise of her relationships with women, and her passions now seem to many modern readers to exceed the norms of romantic friendship:

> Thus our twin-Souls in one shall grow,
> And teach the World new Love,
> Redeem the Age and Sex, and shew
> A Flame Fate dares not move.

As her editor innocently commented in 1667, 'we might well have call'd her the English *Sappho*' (see pp. 44–5). We might well. But where do we draw the line between all these different types of love? And do we have to?

These uncertainties show how impossible it is to impose absolute categorizations, and they also show the diverse forms that love and affection can take. Sexual acts and roles also vary, but these too have often been shaped by societies in rigidly distinct and mutually exclusive ways. Women's desire has sometimes even been assumed not to exist at all, still less been valued and articulated. Women and their lives have often left little evidence in early history compared to the men in power, as will be obvious from the images in this book, which are mostly male. Like all social relationships, love and desire are often bound up with power, status and age. In particular, being a 'real man' has often been viewed as having an exclusively dominant role in all social activities, which means that many cultures have conceived man on man sex in terms of strongly gendered roles. For the 'active' partner, such sex acts did not involve any divergence from acceptable masculine activity and identity, while the 'passive' partner was thought to be taking on the role of a woman and so was breaking the norms. Actions are, of course, not necessarily the same as identity. After all, who is more 'gay', the man who has sex with another man because there is no woman available, or a man who wants to have sex with other men but doesn't because he has a wife? Identities are never simple.

In many societies, sexual acts between men can occur as part of social rituals, such as initiation ceremonies marking the passage from adolescence to adulthood, and so they are often structured by age. Same-sex love has also been presented in more egalitarian terms of comradeship and devotion, as in the Chinese phrase 'the passion of the cut sleeve', recalling a romantic incident in the imperial court. Chinese historians relate that in the Han dynasty, the emperor Ai (ruled 27–1 BC) 'did not care for women'. He loved the married Dong Xian, and bestowed great favours on him as his sexual favourite. In one official history of the period, the writer Ban Gu relates how

> emperor Ai was sleeping in the daytime with Dong Xian stretched out across his sleeve. When the emperor wanted to get up, Dong Xian was still asleep. Because he did not want to disturb him, the emperor cut off his own sleeve and got up. His love and thoughtfulness went this far.

After a failed attempt by the emperor on his death bed to appoint him as his successor, Dong Xian was forced to commit suicide and the Han dynasty ended. But it is said that the incident inspired courtiers to remove their own sleeves, and 'the passion of the cut sleeve' became a way of describing male-male love in Chinese culture. And note that Dong Xian was married. In some societies same-sex desire between men or women has been accepted as long as it did not prevent them from fulfilling the social roles of marrying and having children. It was tolerated but not regarded as a cultural norm or ideal.

Among all this variety, one episode has had notable consequences. Same-sex sexual relationships were prohibited in the Jewish Bible, which tells how God destroyed the wicked city of Sodom with fire after its inhabitants tried to 'know' (an ambiguous word) the angels whom he had sent to visit a virtuous man named Lot. The episode also occurs in the Qur'an. The sins of Sodom were apparently many, but religious tradition has often focused on the same-sex activity that is thought to have been involved, and God's punishment has often been used to justify the persecution of people termed 'sodomites'. The spread of empires has meant that the impact of this interpretation of the tale has been almost worldwide. Often this persecution was part of the political agendas when (Christian) governments colonized other cultures, such as those of South America (see pp. 62–3), although not all Christian religious traditions have been so hostile. The historian John Boswell even claimed that marriage rites between men existed in the early Church, although this has been much disputed.

Past societies equal ours in their self-awareness and complexity, and same-sex desire has often found a means of expression without the modern roles or terms that we would use. The (now standard) terminology of 'homosexual' and 'lesbian' was developed by academics only late in the nineteenth century, and yet individuals' stories show that an awareness of distinctive desires existed well before this. For example, the upper-class Yorkshire woman Anne Lister (1791–1840) (opposite) wrote parts of her extensive diaries in a secret code. These were only published in the 1980s, and in them she shows that she was fully aware that men's admiration was:

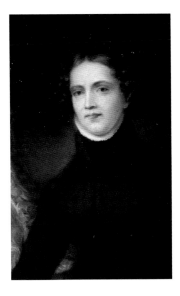

A portrait of Anne Lister by the Yorkshire artist Joshua Horner, from around 1830.

Oil on canvas, 74 x 61 cm.

not meet for me. I love, & only love, the fairer sex & thus beloved by them in turn, my heart revolts from any other love but theirs.

Her masculine appearance and behaviour led her to be mocked as 'Gentleman Jack' by locals, and her affairs with long-term (female) lovers had to be conducted discreetly to avoid public disgrace. Her ability to live her own socially visible life like this was of course only possible because of her comparative wealth and social standing. Her diaries show that desire does not need modern academic terminology in order to exist, and other cultures and periods provide further examples. For instance, the Indian *Kamasutra*, from the fourth century AD, categorizes men who desire other men as having a 'third nature'. In addition, the invisible unrecorded lives of most of the populations of the past may have been more varied than we imagine. Before we label people, we need to understand their cultural world in all its difference and possibilities. As the poet W. H. Auden (1907–73) put it in 1939, more perceptively and concisely than many academics:

> Slowly we are learning,
> We at least know this much,
> That we have to unlearn
> Much that we were taught,
> And are growing chary
> Of emphatic dogmas;
> Love like Matter is much
> Odder than we thought.

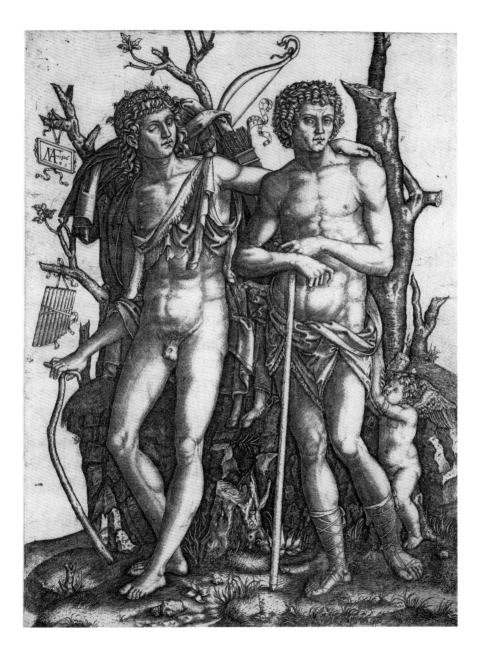

CHANGING ATTITUDES

Attitudes have always varied. Looking through possible historical evidence, different contexts clearly have different rules in every culture. Works of art, for example, will give us a rather different view of the world from legal codes of the same period. An engraving by the Italian artist Marcantonio Raimondi from the early sixteenth century shows the Greek god Apollo with his beloved Hyacynthus (opposite). This was produced in an age when men could be killed for acting on the desires that the print of the affectionate couple evokes and celebrates. As the literary historian Bruce Smith asks, what are we to make of a culture that could produce both such a print and such death sentences? In looking for love in history, we need to remember that art is never simply a reflection of social reality. Much ancient Greek art, both domestic and public, displayed naked male beauty as an image of physical, social and intellectual perfection, even though public male nudity was not common except in athletics grounds. In this case, however, we can be fairly sure that such art had an erotic aspect for the intended (male) viewers. In one of Plato's dialogues from around 390 BC (but set in 432 BC), the philosopher Socrates watches the young aristocrat Charmides, aged around eighteen and judged to be the most handsome Athenian of the moment, as he enters a wrestling school. He is surrounded by admiring men and youths, and 'every one of them looked at him *as if he were a statue*'. Socrates is quick to invite the sexy young man to sit down beside him, but only (he says) so that he can see if his soul is as beautiful and noble as his physique.

It is hard to assess actual lived experiences even from legal records, since laws present a rather simplified view of society and, like Anne Lister, the wealthy could always get away with much that was contrary to how they were supposed to behave.

An engraving by the Italian artist Marcantonio Raimondi, showing Apollo and Hyacynthus. Italy, c. 1510–27.

Paper, 30 x 22.5 cm.

In many societies, openness or indiscretion about sexual habits could perhaps cause more outrage than the sex act itself. When one English gentleman was arrested in the 1840s a friend exclaimed 'Gibson Craig … told me that W[illiam] Bankes had been again caught with a soldier!!! Monstrous madness'. The shock was not so much that he had been with a man, but that he had been caught – and not for the first time (see pp. 82–3). This reaction could turn into panic if the scandal risked implicating the Establishment. The middle-class cross-dressers Ernest Boulton (born 1848) and Frederick Park (born 1847) – known about London as Stella and Fanny – were arrested on 28 April 1870. There was great newspaper coverage and public interest, particularly because one of their partners was a member of the nobility. But then suddenly the press went very quiet. The official reaction to this case involved a double hypocrisy, as the novelist Barbara Ewing notes:

> the hypocrisy of pretending that such sexual practices did not exist (except perhaps among the lower echelons of society) and a further self-seeking hypocrisy: simultaneously working behind the scenes to make sure that some aspects of the case never became public knowledge.

As is clear from such scandals, distinct sub-cultures based on same-sex activities had (unsurprisingly) developed in many societies where there was no significant cultural recognition for same-sex desire or gender diversity. In Europe, these underground cultures probably began from late antiquity onwards. But since these were *sub*-cultures, they are often now difficult to trace. Ironically they are frequently known only from the records created by the very institutions that were attempting to suppress them, and which of course do not

An illustrated ballad, *This is Not the Thing or Molly Exalted*, showing a 60-year-old man being abused in the pillory. Spectators shout 'Flogg him', 'Cut it off'. London, 1762.

Paper, 12.8 x 17 cm.

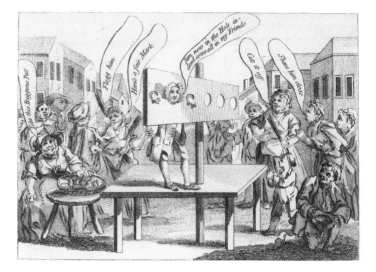

present an unbiased picture. Human society in general, it seems, is very conventional in its attitudes. Sometimes, where 'heterosexual' alliances have been the normal and preferred mode of desire, anything that is less than 'ideal' has been suppressed from the record by governments and religious elites, and even where possible from society itself. Societies have often shown little tolerance of diversity, as is seen in the violent and hostile treatment of effeminate men, known as 'Mollies', in one English broadsheet ballad of 1762 (above):

> Ye Reversers of Nature, each *dear* little Creature,
>   Of soft and effeminate sight,
> See above what your fate is, and 'ere it too late is,
>   Oh, learn to be – all in the *Right*.

English society here enforces its ideas of what is 'natural' and 'right' in a brutal way, ignoring the fact that some other societies have viewed same-sex desire as both natural *and* right.

The laws in Christian Europe were based on values derived from the Bible, but they were not above change. With trade and empire, the West encountered different cultures that indicated that its attitudes towards any sort of sexuality were neither universal nor inevitable. Travellers and historians often viewed sexually explicit objects from other cultures with surprise. New discoveries from the supposedly respectable classical world, such as the Roman city of Pompeii, added to their shock. History showed that same-sex desire did not always necessarily mean anti-social depravity, and the love that had been considered to be 'unspeakable' started to request the right not to be persecuted. After generations of protests and campaigns, attitudes have now changed in many places. In 2011, the US Secretary of State, Hillary Clinton, stated simply that 'gay rights are human rights, and human rights are gay rights'. This change has, however, not always been smooth or easy. Periods of economic hardship or of disease have often made people look

Old and new traditions: a married couple, Olivia and Ying in a romantic setting in Calgary, Alberta.

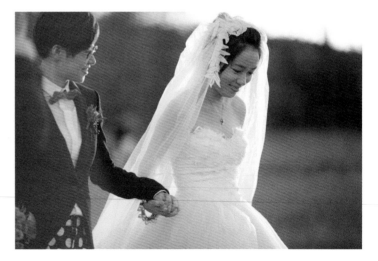

for scapegoats, and foreigners or anyone 'abnormal' and 'different' are always convenient candidates, as during the economic crisis before the Second World War. This vicious tendency of the human animal persists today. In this respect, 'gay' history is very much part of humanity's wider history.

Even in modern times, many people have kept silent about their desires and have not identified themselves in terms of their sexuality. The 'closet' (an image of living secretly) has been hard to escape from. The liberation that has been achieved in many societies over the past century should not be undervalued or taken for granted. In 1963, when I was born, this book could not have been written, and I could not have lived openly with my partner. Even in 2013, this book could not be published in some places: 'homosexuality' is still illegal in around seventy-eight countries across the world, and a death penalty is still applied in five of them. Full legal equality for lesbian, gay, bisexual and transgender people is still very rare, and protests and campaigns for their rights continue. The issue of equal marriage rights in the 2010s is just one specific example of this wider struggle (opposite). As with women's rights, change has nevertheless gathered momentum. Medical advances have even opened up options for transgendered people that were undreamt of a few generations ago. Some parts of the lesbian, gay, bisexual and transgender (LGBT) communities have embraced sexualized identities, very much defined by their sexual preferences, while others embrace identities defined by more domestic concerns and seek assimilation into society. Some want equality and integration, others equality and distinctiveness. Now, many cultures are more ready to recognize that desire can take different forms. For example, the San Francisco novels of Armistead Maupin celebrate a new sort of family and the idea of a person's 'significant other … your spouse and/or lover and/or best buddy'. In many cultures, there are now gay characters in soap operas, gay government ministers, gay historical romances, celebrities who are as open about their gay or pan-sexuality as any 'straight' celebrity, and straight sportsmen who are happy to be gay pin-ups. 'LGBT' people are increasingly visible in increasingly diverse roles. So much so that we may be entering a 'post-gay' age in which sexuality can be an integral part of anyone's identity but need not be contested by anyone else. One day, perhaps everyone will be equal in 'Love, the Beloved Republic'.

'QUEERING' HISTORY

In the 1940s, a famous report on male sexuality by the zoologist Alfred Kinsey (1894–1956) argued that human sexuality was a continuum. He claimed from his sample that ten per cent of the American males surveyed were more or less exclusively 'homosexual' for at least three years between the ages of sixteen and fifty-five. This percentage has been disputed but, regardless of the issues of accuracy or the fact that the sample comes from a single society, this small figure shows why some people regard 'homosexual' experiences as just a 'minority' issue. This view ignores the argument that *all* human sexuality is a continuum, of course, and even this ten per cent seems to represent a rather significant minority, much larger than many people often imagine. And the same is arguably true of the historical past.

Early lesbian, gay, bisexual and transgender histories that were written in the twentieth century often provided a series of positive role models as ancestors for modern 'gay' identity. This type of history is still very powerful, and such famous names often include, as random examples, Alexander the Great,

Socrates, Vergil, Richard the Lion Heart, Leonardo da Vinci, James I, Queen Christina, Frederick the Great, Abraham Lincoln, Walt Whitman, Ludwig Wittgenstein, Alan Turing, Marlene Dietrich and Roland Barthes. The 'gay' side of these famous historical figures was usually not mentioned in official accounts, and these studies performed an important function of regaining a history for people who often felt ignored and suppressed by silence. As a character in Larry Kramer's 1985 play *The Normal Heart* says defiantly, 'I belong to a culture that includes Proust, Henry James, Tchaikovsky, Cole Porter, Plato ...'. Many LGBT people first realize their own sexuality in a moment of recognition that has been inspired by accounts of literary or historical figures – a realization that their feelings are not unique. This process of 'coming out' to oneself and to society has perhaps made it appealing for historians to try to do the same to historical figures and to 'out' them as ancestors and role models. But simply saying such figures are 'gay' underplays the difference of the past, and many scholars feel that it imposes our own modern terminologies and identities a little too freely. But, of course, these figures were certainly not 'heterosexual' either.

In reaction, there has been a movement towards 'queer' history: writing history for those people who are normally excluded (or at least partly suppressed) from the official accounts of the world, and so undermining cultural assumptions about what is 'normal'. 'Queer studies' has moved from trying to identify famous 'homosexuals' in history to tracing the gradual creation of the idea that exclusively 'heterosexual' behaviour is the social and personal norm ('heteronormativity'). 'Queer' was originally a term of abuse for gays as 'abnormal' from the late nineteenth century on, but it has been reclaimed since the 1990s so that it can now describe not only same-sex desire but, in David Halperin's words, '*whatever* is at odds with the normal, the legitimate, the dominant'. Queer readings of history try to analyse the ways in which cultural forces privilege and legitimize what is considered 'normal'. They usefully remind us that all definitions of what is normal or natural are not inevitable, but are instead fictions created by particular societies, and that these fictions need to find things to label 'abnormal' and 'unnatural', against which to define themselves. Such queer readings can be part of a search for histories that include previously excluded groups such as women, children and the poor (so-called 'subaltern histories'). These histories from the bottom up can offer a valuable alternative to the official histories that nation states have often produced – and still produce – for themselves.

Although same-sex desire seems to be present in all societies, some of the examples in this book show how censorship, persecution and simple silence have often written same-sex desire out of history, not only concealing it from contemporaries but also making it inaccessible to historians in the following centuries. In societies where same-sex desire had to live underground, representing itself with ambiguous signals, it was often hard even for a contemporary to be sure what such signs meant. And it is now hugely irritating for a historian who can never read these signals even like someone from that society might have. What did a gesture, an image, a style of clothing mean for people at the time? For example, some nineteenth-century American photographs show men sitting together on each other's laps and embracing in a way that now suggests to many of us a sexually charged intimacy (opposite). But such poses seem not to have necessarily conveyed that message to the original viewers. Is that man, in the words of the playwright Harvey Fierstein, a 'friend friend or a euphemism friend'? As the art historian David Deitcher remarks:

Two pairs of American friends; the names of the photographers and subjects are unknown.

LEFT Quarter-plate daguerrotype photograph, 14.4 x 11.5 cm.

RIGHT Tintype photograph, 9 x 6.4 cm.

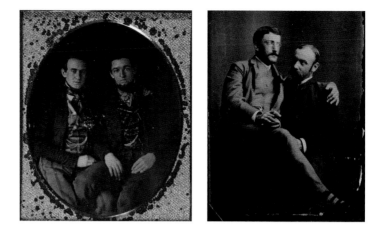

in their elusiveness, their resistance to naming and categorization, such photographs become their own best poetic evidence of the fluidity that marked the relations they reveal but cannot prove.

This is a sign of the continuum of human desire and of our ways of expressing it. It is also a sign of the balancing act that is part of our engagement with the historical other: an unending dialogue between what we recognize as just like us and what we see as different from us. What would it mean if *you* sat on a man's lap like that? What would it have meant twenty years ago, or now but in another country? But among all these cultural uncertainties one thing is reasonably certain: the historical past will have been more varied and 'queerer' than we have often assumed.

Not so long ago, European culture regarded sexuality as something that should not be discussed, especially not in public. Now, however, universities and museums actively research desire and sexuality, often as a means of understanding our

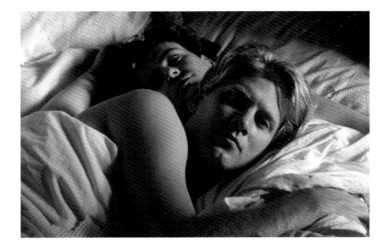

Same-sex romance on a grand scale in a modern work of art. Maurice Hall (James Wilby) and Alec Scudder (Rupert Graves) together in the 1987 film *Maurice* by partners Ismail Merchant and James Ivory. The film was based on E. M. Forster's novel and was partly filmed in the British Museum.

own ways of constructing identity. In 2006, for example, a British Museum special exhibition on the 'Warren Cup' (pp. 50–1) explored ancient attitudes to sexuality. In this, the Roman silver cup showing pairs of men making love was juxtaposed with an image from the 2005 film by Ang Lee, *Brokeback Mountain*. This film explored the love between two cowboys in a homophobic society, and had an immense impact on its audiences. Such a juxtaposition in the displays reminded visitors that same-sex desire has not featured widely in modern European and American culture, in contrast to the art and literature of ancient Greece and Rome. How many romantic films have there been celebrating same-sex love stories compared to those between men and women? And how many with a happy ending, such as E. M. Forster's *Maurice* (above)? Same-sex love has often been relegated to the margins of art as problematic (and preferably tragic), but this is not necessarily the whole story. 'Gay' history is certainly in part a history shaped by persecution and oppression, but same-sex desire has

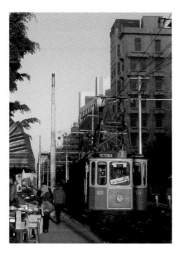

The tramline in the cosmopolitan city of Alexandria where E. M. Forster first met Mohammed el-Adl in 1916. Here a 'great unrecorded history' began.

also been irrepressible and remarkably resistant. As the English novelist E. M. Forster (1879–1970) wrote about his Egyptian lover, Mohammed el-Adl:

> when I am with him, smoking or talking quietly ahead, or whatever it may be, I see, beyond my own happiness and intimacy, occasional glimpses of the happiness of 1000s of others whose names I shall never hear, and know that there is a great unrecorded history.

The sequence of forty or so objects in this book provides a few glimpses of such a history, from across many periods and places. Almost all the objects come from the British Museum, supplemented with some other examples, and we present them within their various cultures in chronological order. We hope that they will not only illustrate some aspects of lesbian, gay, bisexual and transgender history, but will also show the diverse material forms that such history takes. Some objects are directly and unambiguously informative about desire and gender identity, while others speak to us more indirectly. For some periods and cultures it has been hard to find relevant objects, for others much easier. Some cultures, such as the classical Mediterranean or Edo period in Japan, have given same-sex desire prominence in prestigious art forms. Some objects have been valued, some suppressed, some simply not collected by the Museum. The modern history of objects can say much about changing cultural attitudes, as well as shaping the data available for modern historians. Such is the nature of our evidence.

Many of the objects we have chosen are visual representations or texts, because these tend to record desire more directly than many other sorts of object. An undecorated pot cannot tell us about the loves of the people who have handled it. But occasionally objects give us an irreplaceable touch of the real that texts alone cannot provide. On a sheet of Michelangelo's (see pp. 64–5), the combination of the superb drawing and the elegantly written note to his friend, protesting that it is only a first sketch, embodies an infatuated eagerness to impress a young man in a way that feels instantly recognizable to anyone who has ever been in a similar situation. We have tried to include, where possible, contemporary quotes from original voices in order to suggest how the actors perceived their lives, and to evoke specific experiences rather than generalized historical views. It is often surprising how different other cultures are from our own, but it is also surprising how recognizable other people's desires can seem.

Most of all, we would ask you to remember as you read that many other histories are possible. These are just a few pieces – glimpses – of a history as a reminder that diversity is integral to human desire and the whole human condition. Love, desire and gender are never minority concerns.

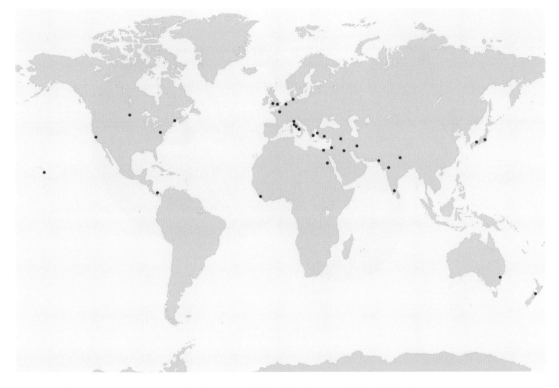

Glimpses of a history across the world: these are the locations featured in the following pages.

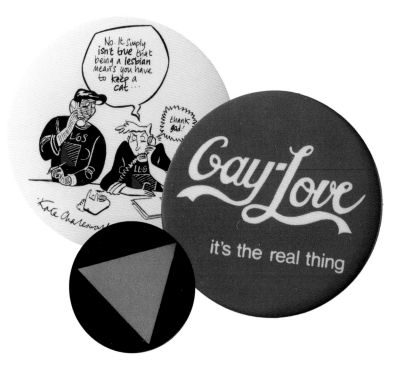

'It gets better'

(Campaign slogan, 2010)

GLIMPSES OF A HISTORY

The Ain Sakhri figures.
Palestine, *c.* 9000 BC.

Calcite, H. 10.2 cm.

EARLY DESIRES?

We may as well begin with a question. This small sculpture, made from a calcite pebble, shows two figures embracing, and is said to have been found in a cave at Ain Sakhri near Bethlehem in modern Palestine. It is the earliest known depiction of a couple making love and is from the Natufian culture, around 11,000 years ago, when hunter-gatherers were beginning to domesticate animals and grains. It is usually assumed to show a man and a woman, but why do we assume this so easily? Nothing makes it absolutely certain that it is a man and a woman: the genders of the figures are unmarked, and the overall shape of the object is extremely phallic, suggesting that it might be concerned as a whole with masculinity. Specialists consider that the figure may be a religious representation of ideas about sexuality and fertility, related to the domestication of the natural world. And so on balance, the two lovers probably are a man and a woman. But they are not necessarily so. This sculpture's ambiguity is a reminder that we should not project our assumptions onto the past. We need not assume that 'hetero-sexuality' or the modern nuclear family as we know them are the default options for any society, ancient or modern. Human history and culture might be much more varied than we imagine.

And looking at any object, it is also worth remembering that we cannot know the desires of the person who once held this flint tool, or used this pot. The everyday intimate histories that surrounded any object are always partly hidden, partly lost, but nevertheless they did once exist. Why should we assume that they *must* have been 'heterosexual'?

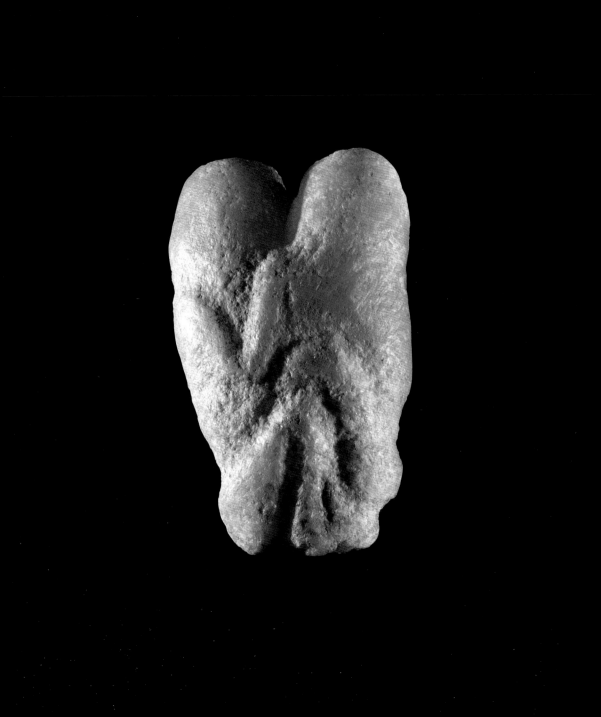

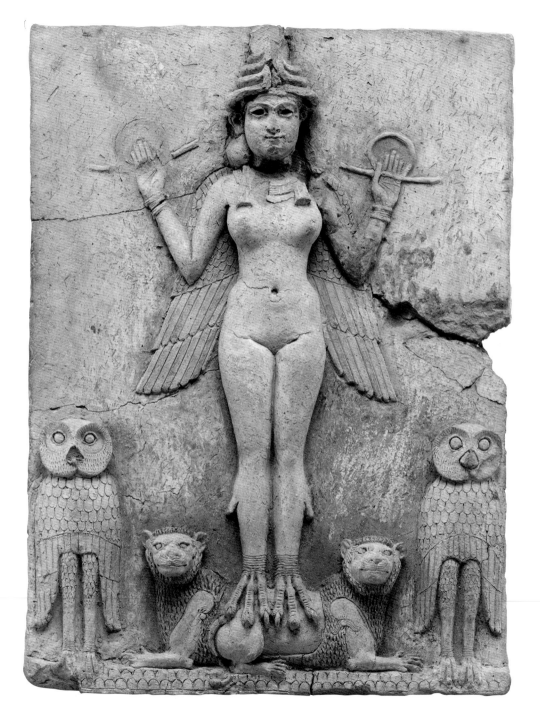

The Mesopotamian panel, now
popularly known as 'The Queen of
the Night', shows a goddess with the
wings and talons of a bird of prey.
c. 1750 BC.

Baked clay, H. 49.5 cm; W. 37 cm; D. 4.8 cm.

A GENDER-CHANGING GODDESS

Gender roles vary between different societies and are not a universal 'given'. Ideas of what it means to be a man or woman can be very different, and many cultures have also envisaged the possibility of a 'third' sex and of changing sex. This baked clay relief panel shows a naked woman wearing the horned headdress characteristic of a deity. She could be an aspect of Ishtar, a goddess of sexual attraction and war, who was also called Inanna in Sumerian. Ishtar could even be shown with a beard in her more warlike forms. She had the power to assign gender identity and could 'change man into woman and woman into man'.

Men called *kurgarru*s were followers of the cult of the goddess, and seem to have been considered woman-like men in some way: the word has been thought by modern scholars to refer to hermaphrodites, eunuchs or 'homosexuals'. In one epic poem, the *kurgarru*s are people

> Whose masculinity Ishtar has turned into
>   femininity to make the people reverend,
> The carriers of dagger, razor, scalpel and flint
>   blades,
> Who regularly do [forbidden things] to delight
>   the heart of Ishtar.

While their sexual identity was obviously regarded as in some way irregular, they were nevertheless part of the divinely ordained world order and of state religion.

LEFT The stela of Hor and Suty, carved with their names, titles and hymns to the sun god. Egypt, *c.* 1375 BC.

Granodiorite, H. 146 cm; W. 90 cm; D. 29 cm.

OPPOSITE Niankhkhnum and Khnumhotep kissing, from their tomb at Saqqara, *c.* 2450 BC.

ANCIENT EGYPTIAN TWINS OR LOVERS?

The Egyptians recognized the existence of same-sex desire, but with different cultural conventions it can be hard to tell whether a representation of male intimacy is an expression of sexual desire or not. There are a few controversial cases from ancient Egypt, including an Old Kingdom tomb dedicated to two male courtiers, Niankhkhnum and Khnumhotep, from around 2450 BC. One scene of the two men embracing has been considered to be the 'first recorded gay kiss', suggesting that they might be the first known socially acknowledged same-sex couple.

This funerary inscription (opposite) poses a similar dilemma. It is dedicated to two male officials, named Hor and Suty, who worked as architects on the temple of Amun at Luxor in around 1375 BC. It has been deliberately damaged, and some scholars have suggested that they were a male couple, whose images were later erased by their outraged wives and children. While this interpretation is technically possible, it is very unlikely because on another inscribed stela (stone tablet) belonging to the men similar erasures include these family members as well. In the inscription each of the men refers to the other as:

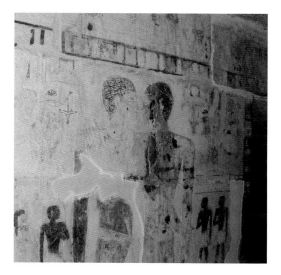

My brother, like myself, whose ways pleased me,
For he had come from the womb
With me on the same day.

This is usually interpreted as meaning that they were twins, and the same is most probably the case with the earlier Niankh-khnum and Khnumhotep. But we know that male couples were a possibility: one poem tells about the scandal caused by a king's affair with his general.

HEROIC LOVE IN MESOPOTAMIA

The famous *Epic of Gilgamesh* tells the story of a semi-historical king, Gilgamesh, and exists in different versions, the main one being composed in the thirteenth to eleventh centuries BC. This Neo-Assyrian copy comes from the royal library of the ruler Ashurbanipal in Nineveh, northern Iraq, from the early seventh century BC. This is a copy of one of twelve tablets that comprised the whole poem. The poet tells how Gilgamesh and the hairy wild man Enkidu become friends. Here, before they meet, Gilgamesh has dreams which are interpreted as meaning that

> A strong partner will come to you,
> One who can save the life of a friend ...
> You will love him as a wife, you will dote on him.

The two virile men have various heroic adventures, but they kill the Bull of Heaven which the goddess Ishtar has sent to punish Gilgamesh for rejecting her advances. Because of this Enkidu dies, and Gilgamesh spends the rest of the poem grieving for his 'friend whom I love so much, who experienced every hardship with me', and trying to outwit death itself.

Such intimacy does not necessarily involve sexual desire, but some historians have debated whether particular words or phrases in their story could have been understood sexually, and whether Gilgamesh and Enkidu were not just friends but lovers. Does this poem celebrate a 'homosocial' relationship or a 'homosexual' one? There is no clear sexual contact between the men, but the relationship is described in erotic terms, making Enkidu a supremely 'significant other' regardless of sex.

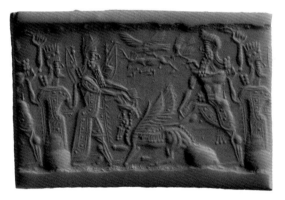

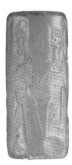

A seal (right) and its clay impression (above) showing the bearded Gilgamesh (on the left) and Enkidu (on the right) killing the Bull of Heaven while Ishtar tries to prevent them. Iraq, eighth century BC.

Chalcedony, H. 2.9 cm; D. 1.3 cm.

A damaged copy of Tablet 1 of
Gilgamesh. Iraq, early seventh
century BC.

Clay, H. 13.7 cm; W. 23.3 cm.

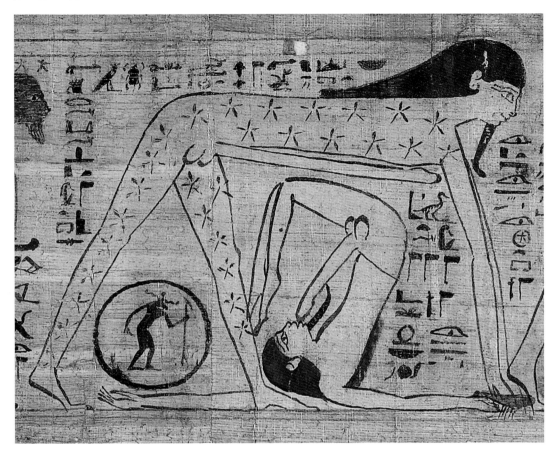

ICONOGRAPHY NOT PORNOGRAPHY

Most of the references to same-sex desire in ancient Egypt are slightly negative: almost all texts and works of art that survive from early cultures are from government or elite circles, and as such present an official ideal view of society made up of happy families. Scenes of fighting boatmen on tomb walls include terms of abuse that they yell at each other, such as 'Back-turner' and 'Fucker', which might take us closer to everyday life. In funerary texts,

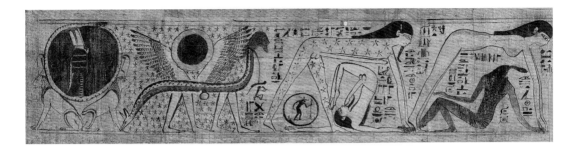

the deceased man says to the gods that he
has never 'had sex with a married woman',
but also that he's never 'had sex with a man
with whom one has sex'.

It is hard to assess what is erotic in another
culture, and even with such a direct visual
image as this papyrus, everything is culturally
shaped. This scene looks like gay pornography
to modern viewers, but it is part of a religious
papyrus from Luxor which was placed in
the burial of a priestess of Amun called
Henuttawy, a member of one of the local
ruling families of the period, around 950 BC.

In it, the cosmos is shown as composed of two
male mythological figures. The lower one is
the earth god Geb who is performing oral
masturbation on himself, apparently to
indicate that the earth is self-sustainingly
fertile. Gods with impressive erections are
very common as symbols of power, strength
and fertility, but this is seen only with the
gods and never in official portrayals of mortal
Egyptian men. Religious iconography can
show things that society does not expect in
everyday life, and actions such as this were
probably not seen in public at the time.

THE LESBIAN POET

In many early societies, women were not prominent in art and culture, and were excluded from public life and politics, apart from domestic and religious rituals. The Greek poet Sappho is said to have lived around 630–570 BC in the town of Mytilene on the isle of Lesbos in the eastern Aegean Sea. Little is known for certain about her life, and ancient accounts are apparently based on imaginative readings of her poems. She seems to have been the head of a socially and religiously sanctioned group of young unmarried girls or women. In a male-dominated society, she gave a voice to women and was regarded as a great and influential poet. This coin dates from the second century AD, when Sappho was already a figure from ancient history, and it was issued in Mytilene, to celebrate its most famous daughter.

Her poems survive only as fragments but they speak directly about desire – and often desire for a woman – in an evocative way:

> Some think a fleet, a troop of horse
> Or soldiery the finest sight
> In all the world; but I say, what one loves.

The female intimacy evoked by many fragments has contributed to the belief that Sappho was a lesbian in the modern sense, and by the late nineteenth century her poetry had made the word for an inhabitant of Lesbos into a word for a woman who loves women. She has been – and remains – an inspirational figure. As she herself said:

> I'm sure that people will remember us.

On one side of the coin (left) is Sappho's head with her name, on the other (below) the words '[the people of] Mytilene' and a poet's lyre, the emblem of the city. Greece, second century AD.

Copper alloy, Diam. 2 cm.

OPPOSITE A fragmentary papyrus with some of Sappho's poems, first identified in 2004. Egypt, third century BC.

Papyrus, H. 17 cm; W. 11.5 cm.

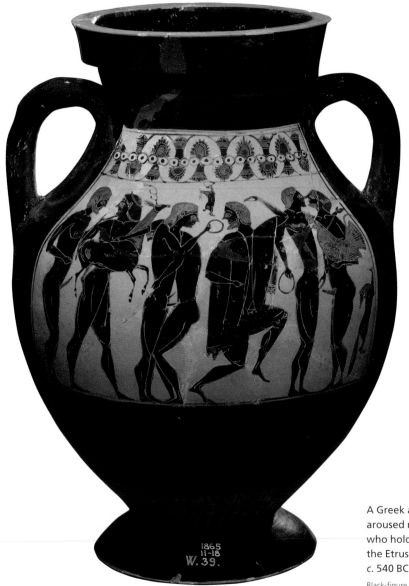

A Greek amphora showing
aroused men with young athletes
who hold wreaths, exported to
the Etruscan city of Vulci in Italy.
c. 540 BC.

Black-figure pottery, H. 34.5 cm; W. 26 cm.

GREEK MEN TOGETHER

Intimacy between men was culturally approved in some city states in ancient Greece. Sexual relationships between males were famously celebrated in Athens in the fifth to fourth centuries BC. Like most social relationships there, these were structured by age, and the ideal beloved was a young man around eighteen or nineteen years old, but there is also evidence for long lasting relationships between older men. Erotic scenes could decorate drinking cups and other domestic vessels. This large Greek vase was painted in Athens around 540 BC and shows bearded men courting athletic youths with love-gifts of animals, and also having sex between their thighs.

On a later Athenian wine cup from around 485–480 BC, men recline on garlanded couches and are served by boys. They drink wine from cups exactly like this one, in a homoerotic atmosphere, charged with the possibility of sex. This wealthy male world was the setting for Plato's *The Symposium* (*The Drinking Banquet*), a dialogue written around 380 BC on the nature of love, featuring the philosopher Socrates (469–399 BC). In this, love is implicitly between men, and in one speech the Athenian aristocrat Phaedrus says

> There can be no greater benefit for a boy than to have a lover from his earliest youth, nor for a lover to have a worthy object for his affection … If then one could contrive that a state or an army should consist entirely of lovers and loved, it would be impossible for it to have a better organization … a handful of such men, fighting side by side, would defeat practically the whole world.

A Greek wine cup with a drinking banquet scene, also exported to the Etruscan city of Vulci in Italy. c. 485–480 BC.

Red-figure pottery, H. 12.7 cm; Diam. 31.75 cm.

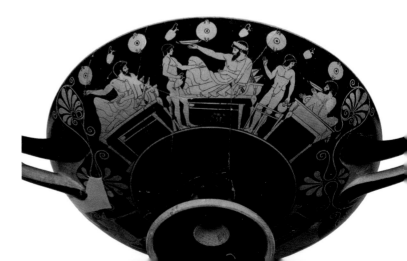

ITALIAN SEDUCTIONS

This lavish marble wellhead is said to have come from the island of Capri. It is decorated with four aroused males pursuing their reluctant objects of desire: three of these are women and one is a youth. One man is the hero Hercules who, while he was a slave of the legendary Lydian queen Omphale, had to wear women's clothes, while she wore his butch lion-skin cloak. Here he reasserts his virility and she resists (but they later married). The other scenes show the mythological world of the highly sexed satyrs and maenads, followers of the god of wine, who symbolize the wild forces of nature. Under a tree, a bearded man grabs the arm of a youth who is holding a set of pipes. This youth may be a shepherd, evoking the amorous idyllic world of pastoral poetry, although this scene is well known in other variations which show a satyr grabbing a hermaphrodite.

These scenes suggest how man on man sex was just another sort of desire in the Roman world, provided that a Roman man remained the active partner. Erotic scenes were not unusual as decorative motifs in domestic contexts, although this wellhead might have come from the gardens on Capri of the private villa of the emperor Tiberius (ruled AD 14–37), who was notorious for his voyeuristic,

pan-sexual tastes. In contrast, when the wellhead was first displayed in the private collection of Charles Townley (1737–1805) in his London house in the 1790s, it seems that the male-male scene was carefully hidden against a wall.

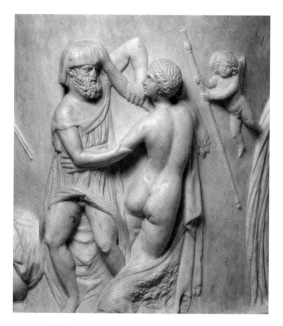

ABOVE The hero Hercules, dressed as a woman, assaults the queen Omphale.

OPPOSITE Wellhead depicting a satyr grabbing a youth and pushing a foot up between his legs as he tries to escape. Italy, late first century BC.

Marble, H. 81.3 cm; W. 78.7 cm.

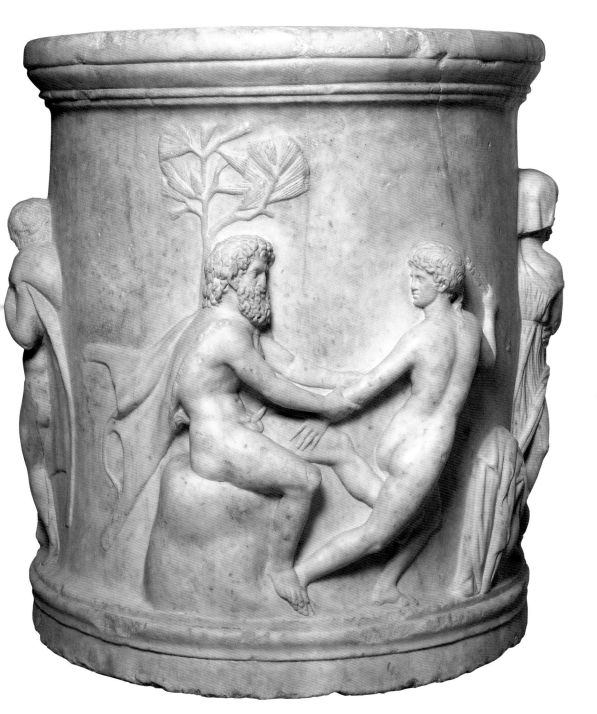

The 'Warren Cup' showing a scene of an older couple, watched by a peeping slave. Palestine, c. AD 10.

Silver, H. 11 cm (max.); Diam. 11 cm (max.).

THE 'WARREN CUP'

This silver drinking cup, now without its handles, probably dates to late in the reign of the emperor Augustus (ruled 27 BC–AD 14). On one side, a bearded man is having sex with a beardless youth, and on the other side, a beardless youth is having sex with a younger male. Such scenes of a young man with a teenager (probably between fourteen and sixteen years old) are now highly controversial, but in Roman society the age difference was part of what made the relationship acceptable, and youth is, of course, often highly valued in many cultures.

The Romans considered that a man should be dominant, both socially and sexually, and as long as he was dominant he retained a proper masculine role and status, but reality will have been much more varied; there is even evidence for marriages between men. Another boy, probably himself a slave, looks in at the door and observes the sensuous and tender scene, just as we are doing. This luxurious drinking cup is likely to have been commissioned by wealthy members of a Greek community, perhaps in one of the major cities of the eastern Mediterranean.

The cup was said to have been found at Bittir, close to Jerusalem, and was bought by the American art collector Edward Perry Warren (1860–1928), who lived with his friend (and probably lover) John Marshall (1862–1928) in Lewes in Sussex, where he tried to recreate a classical style of life. He referred to the cup as the 'Holy Grail' and treasured its direct portrayal of same-sex desire. In 1999 it was acquired by the British Museum, who had not purchased it earlier in the 1950s when 'homosexuality' was still illegal in Britain. It has been on public display ever since.

The younger couple on the other side of the 'Warren Cup'.

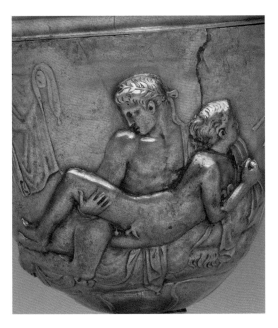

GLIMPSES OF WOMEN TOGETHER

In the surviving brothel and public baths in the Roman seaside city of Pompeii, wall paintings show various types of sex act, and one scene in the so-called Suburban Baths seems to show two women together. Such scenes are rare, but this first-century oil lamp from Roman Turkey shows two women having oral sex together on a couch. While sex was often shown on everyday items, it is uncertain who would have used or seen this lamp. It may have been made to titillate male viewers, rather than to appeal to women. This is a recurrent problem with many representations of same-sex desire between women in male-dominated societies.

Woman on woman sex was the exact opposite of socially accepted gender roles in Roman society, and was condemned and mocked by many authors, such as the Greek writer Lucian (AD 115–80). In one of his comic dialogues, a courtesan tells her friend Leaena that

> we've been hearing strange things about you Leaena. They say that Megilla ... is in love with you just like a man, that you live with each other, and do goodness knows what together.

Leaena blushes and admits that she has been seduced by this rich woman from Lesbos, who had renamed herself with the man's name Megillos, had married a woman and had a shaven head like an athlete. Her friend comments that she must be

> a sort of woman for the ladies. They say there are women like that in Lesbos, with faces like men, and unwilling to consort with men, but only with women, as though they themselves were men.

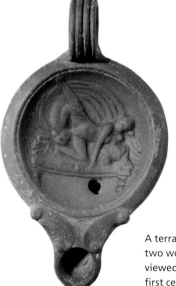

A terracotta lamp depicting two women having oral sex, viewed from above. Turkey, first century AD.

Terracotta, Diam. 7.8 cm.

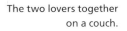

The two lovers together
on a couch.

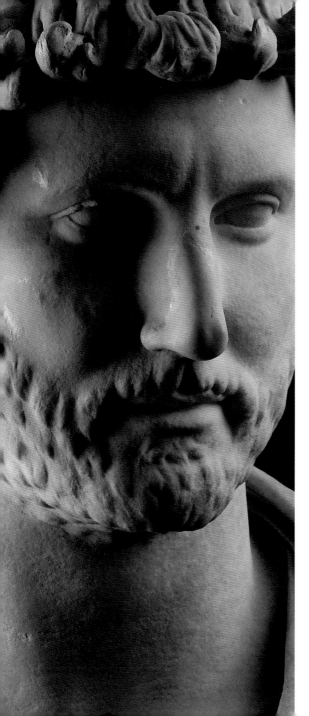

AN IMPERIAL ROMANCE

The reign of the emperor Hadrian (ruled AD 117–38) was marked by military campaigns and imperial building projects, including the famous wall across the north of England at the edge of the Roman Empire. Hadrian had married into the imperial family, but in his late forties he met a Greek youth named Antinous from Bithynia, now in modern Turkey, possibly during a tour of that province in AD 123. The young man became the emperor's lover. During an imperial tour of Egypt in AD 130, according to an ancient biography,

> while he was sailing on the Nile he lost his Antinous, for whom he wept like a woman. About this there are various rumours, some claiming that he had devoted himself to death for Hadrian's sake, others claiming what his physique and also Hadrian's sensuality suggest [i.e. that he was growing too old for the emperor's desire].

Hadrian founded a city named Antinoopolis at the place where his lover died, and made him into a god – an honour usually reserved for members of the emperor's family. Hadrian publicly commemorated Antinous in huge numbers of statues, figures, portraits and coins across the known Roman world, an almost unparalleled public memorial to a lost love. An inscription on an Egyptian-style obelisk erected in Antinous' honour proclaims that he was

A youth, fair of face who makes eyes bright ...
Whose heart rejoiced like a hero's
When he received the order of the gods at the
time of his death.

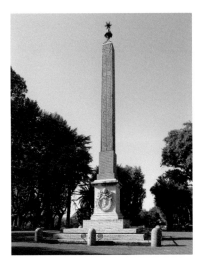

ABOVE The obelisk for the deified Antinous, now in the gardens of the Monte Pincio in Rome, c. AD 130.

RIGHT A head of Antinous from Rome, after AD 130.
Marble, H. 81 cm.

OPPOSITE A bust of Hadrian from his villa at Tivoli, c. AD 117–18.
Marble, H. 84 cm.

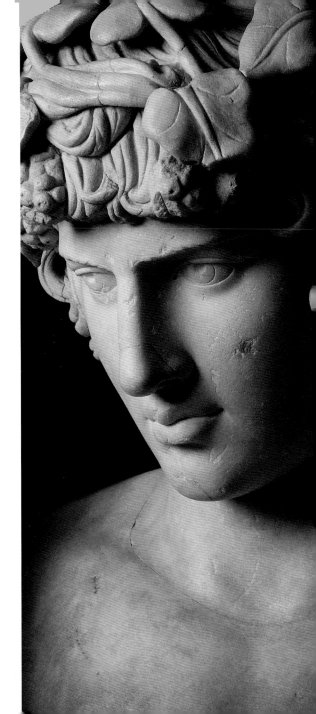

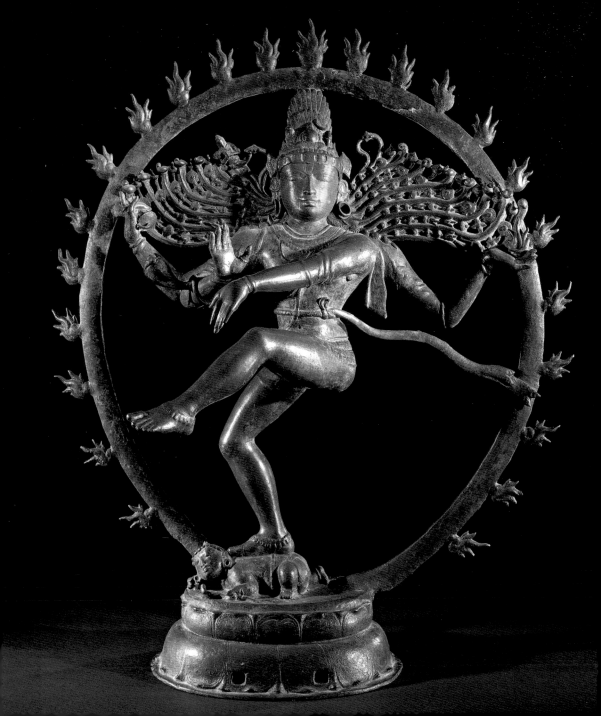

A LORD OF THE DANCE

In many cultures, sex is sacred and can be an image of cosmic creation and fertility. One tradition of art and architecture in India includes scenes of sex on temple walls, a very small number of which show same-sex couples. In Hindu mythology gender is often fluid, with the divine transcending any mortal categories of male and female.

The male god Shiva embodies creative and destructive principles that can be represented by the image of a cosmic dance, marking the end of one cycle of world history and the beginning of another. Here, he dances on the demon Apasmara who is under his right foot, symbolizing his triumph over ignorance. This figure from Tamil Nadu, superbly cast in a copper alloy, is not an erotic work of art, but would have been paraded through the streets in festival processions. The deity's sexual inclusiveness is subtly indicated by his differently shaped earrings (one is masculine in style, the other feminine).

Hindu sacred texts exalt same-sex friendship, as well as 'heterosexual' desire, as an image of the relationship between a god and his devotee, and include myths of gods changing gender and of same-sex divine couples giving birth to children. At least in principle, such diversity has been accepted as a possibility in human society too, despite the high value placed on marriage and procreation. As two modern Indian historians note:

> at most times and places in pre-nineteenth century India love between women and between men, even when disapproved of, was not actively persecuted. As far as we know, no one has ever been executed for homosexuality in India.

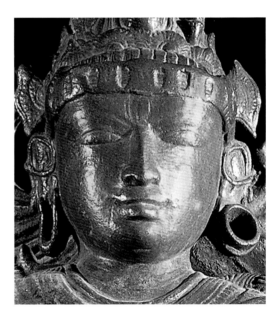

ABOVE **The two styles of earring.**

OPPOSITE Shiva, the dancing god. India, *c.* 1100.
Copper alloy, H. 89.5 cm.

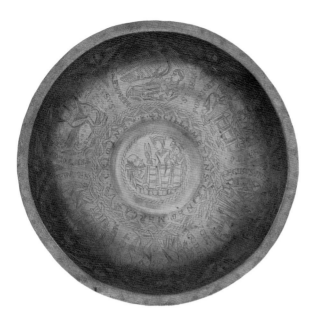

LEFT The 'Scylla Bowl', viewed from above, and (below left) a detail showing 'Jove's eagle carrying off Ganymede'. Germany, twelfth century.

Bronze, Diam. 25.8 cm.

BELOW Ganymede looking affectionately at the eagle of Jove in a Roman statue. Italy, second century AD.

Marble, H. 87.6 cm.

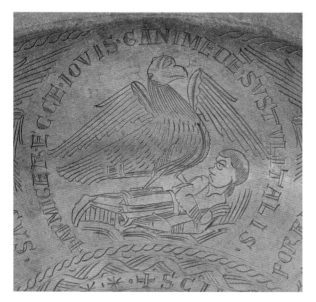

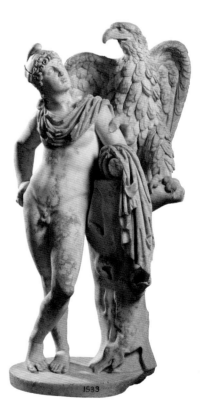

RAPE OR RAPTURE

As Christianity spread through late antique Europe, images from classical culture continued to be produced, although beliefs had changed. This twelfth-century bowl is one of two found at Hawbridge in Gloucestershire, Britain. It was possibly made in Germany, and is presumably from an elite household or religious establishment. It is decorated with pagan mythological scenes, and one shows Jove as an eagle carrying off the young man Ganymede to have sex with him. To the right of this, Ganymede is shown acting as cupbearer to Jove and his wife in heaven. These scenes of the myth of Ganymede are very different from Roman versions, and embody the attitudes of the new religion towards human sexuality. Ganymede is now fully clothed and looks rather unhappy as he is grabbed by the eagle, whereas in classical art he is usually a sensuously naked youth who seems fully aware of Jove's erotic intentions.

The myth was often allegorized, and Ganymede appears in moralized form in some medieval sources as an image of the virtuous soul ascending to god. 'Ganymede' is found as a term describing same-sex relationships in monasteries, where some writers celebrated passionate male-male friendships, but not sexual activity, which was a crime. The word was also used as a term of abuse, and was applied to people such as the much later London bookseller and jeweller Samuel Drybutter. He was notorious for his sexual tastes, and although he repeatedly escaped being convicted for sodomy, he was beaten to death by a London mob in 1777.

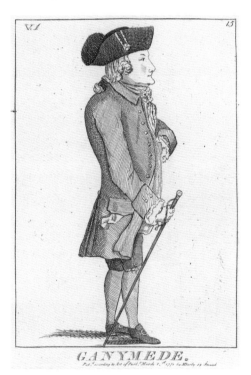

A satirical print of Samuel Drybutter, published by Matthew Darly. London, 1771.

Paper, 15.3 x 10.4 cm.

A MEDIEVAL SINNER

Christian and Jewish attitudes to sexuality stressed procreation, and condemned same-sex desire as against nature and therefore worthy of damnation. The term 'sodomy', from the biblical story of the divine destruction by fire of the godless town of Sodom, covered many practices often deemed irregular and unnatural (including simply masturbation), and it could carry the death penalty in some parts of medieval Europe.

Divine judgement is seen in *The Divine Comedy* by the Florentine poet Dante Alighieri (1265–1321). In this, Dante travels through hell, purgatory and heaven while alive, guided by the spirit of the Roman poet Vergil. In the third ring of the seventh circle of Hell, Dante meets his dead teacher and guardian, the Florentine poet Brunetto Latini (around 1220–94) with people who are

> All clerks and great men of letters, and of
> great fame,
> Defiled in the world by the very same sin.

The unnamed 'same sin' is sodomy, and their eternal punishment is to run incessantly through a rain of fire, as shown in this print where the two travellers stand by a stream overlooking a sandy waste inhabited by the

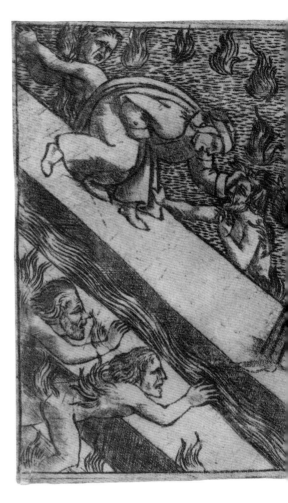

damned. Love is the central theme of the poem, and even here Dante stands a little apart from his guide to speak affectionately to the spirit of Brunetto Latini.

The Divine Comedy is the most enduring work of Italian literature, and has been much

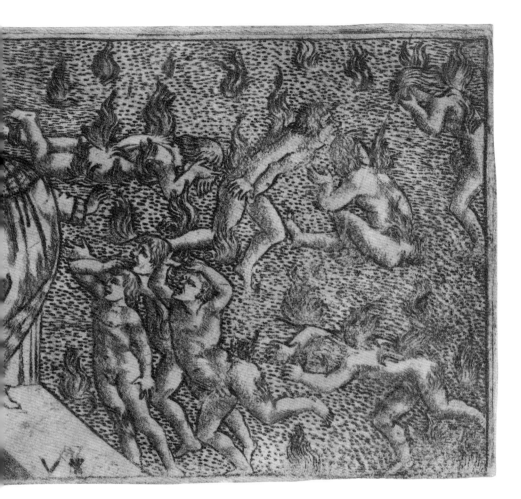

illustrated. This print, attributed to Baccio Baldini (1436–87), was made later in the Italian Renaissance, around 1484–7. It is after a design by the famous Florentine artist Sandro Botticelli (1445–1510), who was himself accused of sodomy.

The fiery landscape of *Inferno*, canto 15, with Dante bending down to Latini. Attributed to Baccio Baldini. Italy, *c.* 1484–7.

Paper, 9.6 x 17.5 cm.

'NEW' WORLDS

When Europeans encountered the 'new' world of the Americas, they met very different societies and different gender roles. Any evidence of what colonists called 'sodomy' could be used to justify violence against the indigenous population, and in 1519 the invading Spanish conquistador Hernán Cortés (1485–1547) declared – very conveniently –

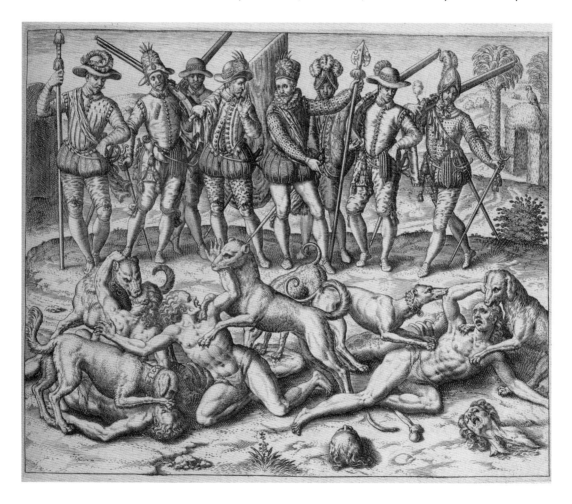

that 'they are all sodomites'.

The explorer Vasco Nuñez de Balboa (1475–1519) is well known for crossing the Isthmus of Panama and for being the first European to see the Pacific Ocean from the Americas. Two days before arriving at the Pacific on 5 October 1513, he encountered the brother of an Indian ruler with many young men dressed as women. He commanded that they be fed to his dogs for what he regarded as their 'unnaturall lechery'. Published accounts of Balboa's achievements were later illustrated in 1594 by the Flemish artist Theodore de Bry (1528–98). His print shows long-haired Panamanian Indians being ripped to pieces by the dogs, watched by a row of the courtly soldiers who visually represent an orderly version of European male culture in contrast to the disorderly 'sodomites'.

In indigenous American societies cross-dressing was common, and some important pre-Columbian deities have male and female attributes in both oral accounts and visual representations. In Mexico, for example among the Mexica (Aztecs) and Huastecs, the goddess of filth and sexual excess, Tlazolteotl, was in some incarnations represented as a woman warrior with both female and male characteristics. Original sources are, unsurprisingly, hard to find since the colonial regimes destroyed many indigenous manuscripts and statues.

OPPOSITE **Theodore de Bry, *Balboa Feeding Several Indians who Had Committed the Terrible Sin of Sodomy to the Dogs to Have them Torn to Pieces*. Germany, 1594.**

Paper, 16.1 x 19.8 cm.

BELOW **A Huastec statue of the goddess Tlazolteotl. Mexico, before 1521.**

Sandstone, H. 150 cm; W. 57 cm; D. 14 cm.

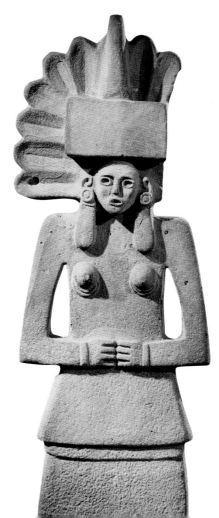

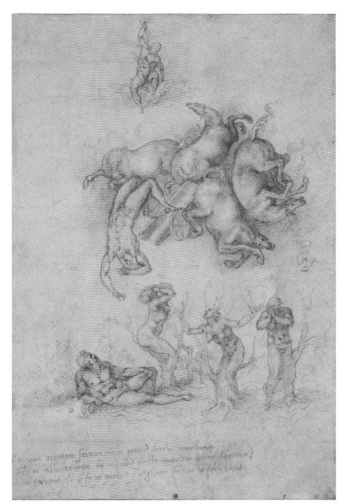

THE 'DIVINE' PRISONER

In Renaissance Florence, young unmarried men often had sexual relations with other men, usually structured by age, with as many as two-thirds of all men being at one time accused of being 'sodomites'. Unlike most Florentines, the great artist, the 'divine'

Michelangelo Buonarroti (1475–1564) remained unmarried, and his art embodies a consistent attraction to the adult male physique, although his contemporary biographers stressed that he was single, chaste and virtuous. In 1532, when nearly sixty, he met the young Roman nobleman Tommaso de'Cavalieri (1509–87) and fell in love. His sonnets written to Cavalieri declare his passionate infatuation:

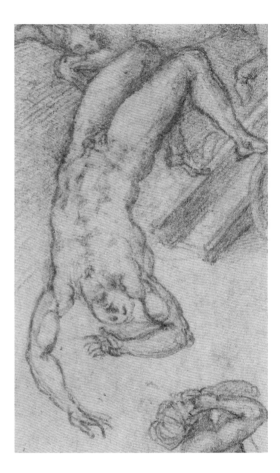

> If I must be conquered and chained to be happy,
> It's no wonder that I, naked and alone, remain
> The prisoner of an armoured knight ['cavalier
>   armato' or beloved cavalieri].

Michelangelo also presented him with drawings as private gifts. This sheet, the first version of one present, was sent to Cavalieri with an eager note at the bottom of the drawing:

> Tom, if this sketch does not please you, say so
> to Urbino [Michelangelo's servant] so that I
> have time to do another by tomorrow evening
> as I promised you; and if it pleases you and
> you want me to finish it, send it back to me.

His friendship with the young nobleman was well known and occasionally mocked, and it continued after Cavalieri's marriage and until Michelangelo's death.

Michelangelo has often been a touchstone for modern gay male identity. Some of his sonnets to Cavalieri were set to music by the British composer Benjamin Britten (1913–76) in the early 1940s for his partner Peter Pears (1910–86) to sing.

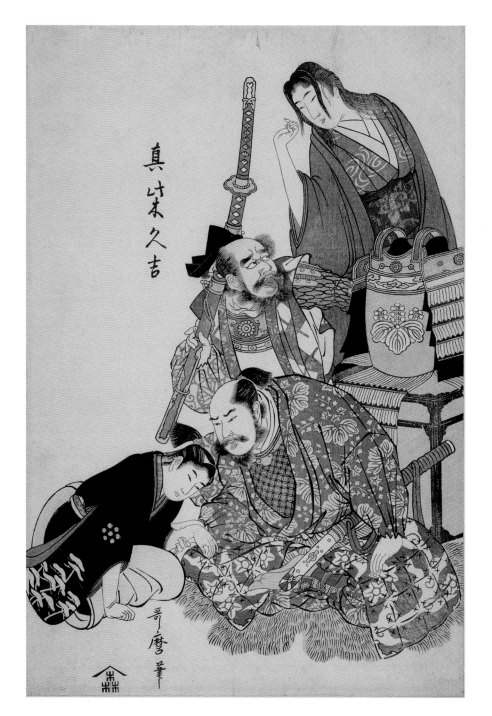

真柴久吉

哥麿筆

LOVE AMONG WARRIORS

In Japan, religious beliefs did not lead to persecution, and male-male love was culturally valued. The world of the elite warrior class, the samurai, centred around male honour. This masculine ethos favoured relationships between warriors and their younger pages, and erotic relationships were embedded in many aspects of warrior culture. The eighteenth-century *Book of the Samurai* comments that

> to lay down one's life for another is the basic principle of *shudō* (male love). If it is not so, it becomes a matter of shame.

Shudō is abbreviated from *wakashudō* 'the way of youths', and such relationships were usually age structured. Although celebrated in writing and art, such erotic behaviour was also carefully regulated by government laws.

Hashiba Hideyoshi (1536–98) was a famous general and warrior, and this wood-block print by the artist Kitagawa Utamaro (died 1806) is one of a group showing him together with his (female) concubines. Each design features one or two women in the composition and is lightly comic in tone. This print shows Hideyoshi reassuringly holding the hand of his young page-boy Ishida Mitsunari (1560–1600), who was later a distinguished samurai in his own right and a minister in Hideyoshi's government. The tenderness

of these two figures perhaps contrasts with the pair behind them: there, another warrior seems to be pestering a woman with his unwanted attentions. The sequence of prints as a whole was thought to insult the historical Hideyoshi's dignity, and Utamaro was punished in 1804 with a sentence of fifty days in handcuffs for this and other related publications.

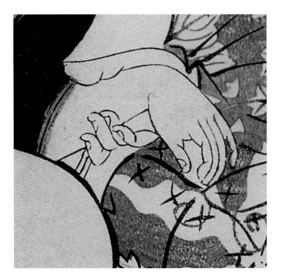

OPPOSITE **Kitagawa Utamaro,** *Mashiba Hisayoshi.* **A controversial view of a historical figure. Japan, 1804.**

Woodblock print on paper, 38 x 25.5 cm.

ABOVE **A tender gesture.**

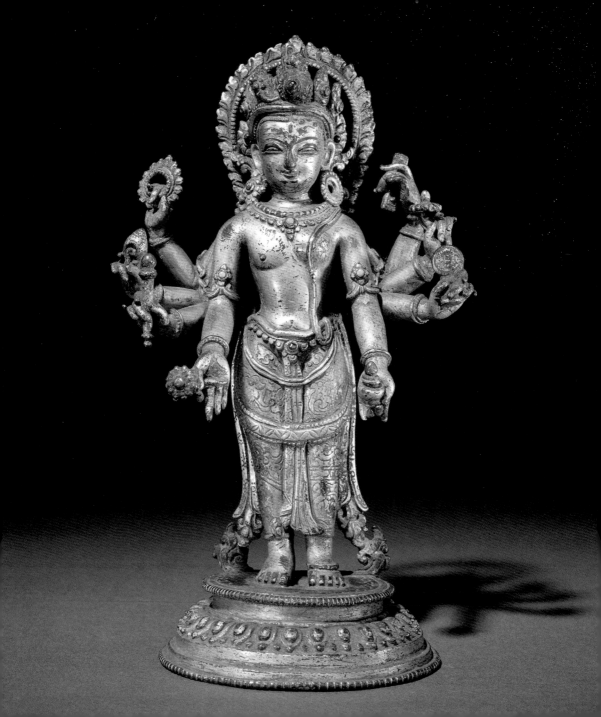

Lakshminarayan, a figure of two
in one. Nepal, seventeenth century.

Gilded bronze, inlaid with turquoise and a
precious stone, H. 14.5 cm.

DIVINE ANDROGYNY

Androgyny, the combination of male and female characteristics, occurs in many religious traditions around the world. Many tribal peoples manifest this notion in the cross-dressing of ritual specialists such as shamans. In most instances, divine androgyny is used to express metaphorically notions of the complementarity of male and female and the ability of the gods to transcend such categories. In Indian culture, concepts of gender and identity were described in philosophical and religious literature such as the *Rig Veda* from around 1500 BC.

The Hindu deity Lakshminarayan represents the male god Vishnu and his female consort Lakshmi, and he is sometimes shown as a single figure whose body is half male and half female. The deity stands on a lotus, and the left side is feminine, while the right side is masculine. The differing characteristics have been subtly indicated in details such as the single female breast, the different earrings and the different pleatings of the *dhoti* – the male side (right) terminates with a zig-zag motif, while the female side (left) sweeps away gracefully from the centre line. This seventeenth-century figure is made of gilded bronze, and inlaid with turquoise. Most images of this type come from Nepal, where Hinduism and Buddhism have been practised side by side, often in distinctive and combined forms.

This concept is also found in the more frequently depicted figure of Ardhanarisvara, who represents the god Shiva and his female consort Parvati. In one myth Shiva even has sex with Vishnu in the form of a woman, producing a son.

Seemes feeing, but effectually is out:
For it no forme deliuers to the heart
Of bird, of flowre, or shape which it doth lack,
Of his quick obiects hath the minde no part,
Nor his owne vision houlds what it doth catch:
For if it fee the rud'st or gentlest fight,
The most fweet-fauor or deformedst creature,
The mountaine, or the fea, the day, or night:
The Croe, or Doue, it shapes them to your feature.
　Incapable of more repleat, with you,
　My most true minde thus maketh mine vntrue.

114

OR whether doth my minde being crown'd with you
　Drinke vp the monarks plague this flattery?
Or whether shall I fay mine eie faith true,
And that your loue taught it this *Alcumie?*
To make of monsters, and things indigest,
Such cherubines as your fweet selfe refemble,
Creating euery bad a perfect best
As fast as obiects to his beames affemble:
Oh tis the first, tis flatry in my feeing,
And my great minde most kingly drinkes it vp,
Mine eie well knowes what with his gust is greeing,
And to his pallat doth prepare the cup.
　If it be poifon'd, tis the leffer finne,
　That mine eye loues it and doth first beginne.

115

THofe lines that I before haue writ doe lie,
　Euen thofe that faid I could not loue you deerer,
Yet then my iudgement knew no reafon why,
My most full flame should afterwards burne cleerer.
But reckening time, whofe milliond accidents
Creepe in twixt vowes, and change decrees of Kings,
Tan facred beautie, blunt the sharp'st intents,
Diuert strong mindes to th' courfe of altring things:
Alas why fearing of times tiranie,

Might

Might I not then fay now I loue you best,
When I was certaine ore in-certainty,
Crowning the present, doubting of the rest:
　Loue is a Babe, then might I not fay fo
　To giue full growth to that which still doth grow.

119

LEt me not to the marriage of true mindes
　Admit impediments, loue is not loue
Which alters when it alteration findes,
Or bends with the remouer to remoue.
O no, it is an euer fixed marke
That lookes on tempests and is neuer shaken;
It is the star to euery wandring barke,
Whofe worths vnknowne, although his higth be taken.
Lou's not Times foole, though rofie lips and cheeks
Within his bending fickles compaffe come,
Loue alters not with his breefe houres and weekes,
But beares it out euen to the edge of doome:
　If this be error and vpon me proued,
　I neuer writ, nor no man euer loued.

117

ACcufe me thus, that I haue fcanted all,
　Wherein I should your great deferts repay,
Forgot vpon your dearest loue to call,
Whereto al bonds do tie me day by day,
That I haue frequent binne with vnknown mindes,
And giuen to time your owne deare purchaf'd right,
That I haue hoysted faile to al the windes
Which should transport me farthest from your fight,
Booke both my wilfulneffe and errors downe,
And on iust proofe surmise, accumilate,
Bring me within the leuel of your frowne,
But shoote not at me in your wakened hate:
　Since my appeale faies I did striue to prooue
　The constancy and virtue of your loue

H　118

A page opening of *Shake-speares Sonnets, Never before Imprinted*, with Sonnet 116. London, 1609.

Paper, H. 21 cm; W. 27.5 cm.

SHAKESPEAREAN LOVE

In early modern England, women were not allowed to act in the public theatre, and so women's roles were taken by boys, most famously in the plays of William Shakespeare (1564–1616). His comedies explore themes of cross-dressing and gender ambiguity, almost suggesting that gender is constructed by circumstances. 'Call me Ganymede' says one boy actor playing a girl who is disguised as a boy who will mock-woo the man she really loves, raising the issue of ambiguous sexuality. In the final scene they marry as man and wife, but the joyful, confusing performance of gender and desire remains the heart of the comedy.

Shakespeare's sequence of 154 sonnets is mostly addressed by the poet to a man, while some of the poems are to a mistress. They were first published in 1609, but in a later edition of 1640 many of the masculine pronouns were changed to feminine, creating the impression that these poems were addressed to a woman.

The sonnets have often been felt to be slightly scandalous, with their talk of the 'the master-mistress of my passion', and have raised questions as to whether Shakespeare was in modern terms 'bisexual'. They give a sense of private and intense sexual feelings, and sometimes of a sublime love:

> Let me not to the marriage of true minds
> Admit impediments. Love is not love
> Which alters when it alteration finds …

It is of course impossible to guess an author's private life from reading his fictional works, but it is noteworthy that some of the greatest love poetry written in English is apparently by a man to a man.

'Love', a familiar word with multiple meanings in different places and different times.

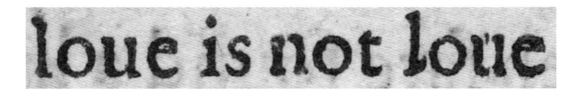

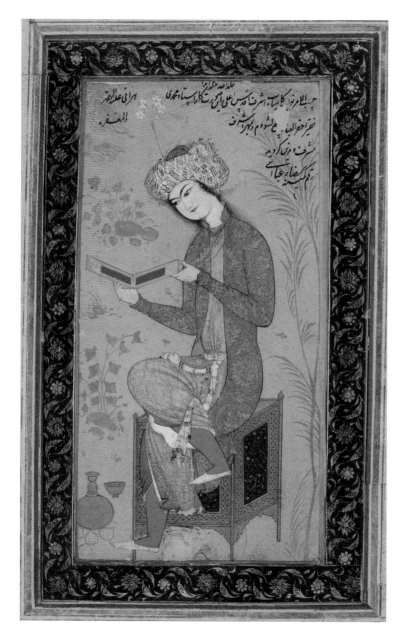

LEFT A gilded youth reading a book of poetry, painted by Riza-yi 'Abbasi. Iran, 1625–6.

Opaque watercolour, gold and ink on paper, 14.5 x 8 cm (excluding border).

OPPOSITE A painting of Shah Abbas with a page, by Muhammad Qasim. Iran, 1627.

Ink drawing with coloured and gold highlights on paper, 25.5 x 15 cm.

PAGES FROM THE PERSIAN COURT

Islam, like the other Abrahamic religions Judaism and Christianity, has often been hostile to same-sex desire, but there are also traditions of tolerance, as in the verses of the poet Abu Nuwas (757–814) who celebrated his love of wine and young men:

> I saw the boy in the darkness and embraced him –
> O would that this kissing could last!

And Persian Sufi religious poetry has often presented the longing of the soul for god in homoerotic terms.

In every society, high rank provides a certain freedom, as with Shah Abbas I (1571–1629) who ruled Iran. He was famous even in Europe for his political, military and religious achievements. He was brilliant and ruthless (killing or blinding his sons), but was also fond of young men. This painting shows a lavishly dressed youth sitting reading a book of poetry. It was painted in the cosmopolitan royal city of Isfahan, and the Persian caption indicates that it was painted under the patronage of Shah Abbas himself:

> On the order of the prosperous, most noble, most pure Highness, may God prolong his reign ... the work of the humble Riza-yi 'Abbasi.

The ruler's romantic interest in young men is more explicit in another painting of 1627 which shows him embracing a young page who is serving him wine under a tree by a stream. This might also come from the ruler's own collections, and an accompanying poem reads:

> May the world fulfil your wishes from three lips,
> The lips of the beloved, the lips of the stream and
>   the lips of a cup.

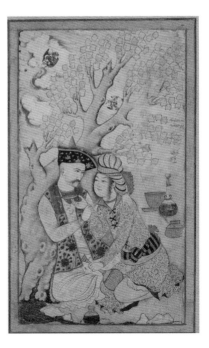

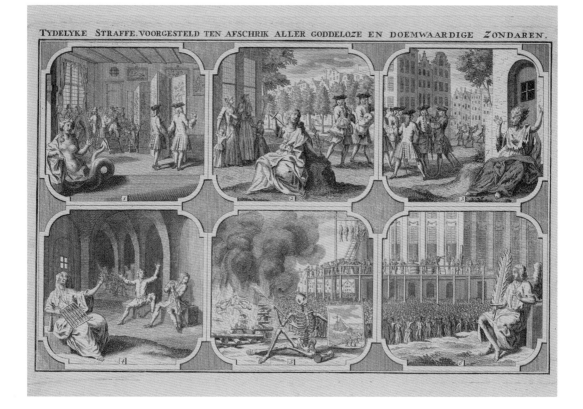

TYDELYKE STRAFFE, VOORGESTELD TEN AFSCHRIK ALLER GODDELOZE EN DOEMWAARDIGE ZONDAREN.

EXECUTING SODOMITES

In the eighteenth century, despite the persecution of same-sex desire in Christian Europe, there was a growing sense that sexual acts between men could be signs of a distinctive and sometimes exclusive identity. In 1730, seventy-five men were executed in the Netherlands because of their activities with other men. In the following eighty years, up to a thousand trials were held, and the records of these reveal evidence for a sub-culture with special 'cruising grounds' and taverns where such men could meet.

This broadsheet (a public poster with announcements or advertisements) is from

1730 and entitled *This-worldly Punishment Represented to Deter all Godless and Damnable Sinners*. At the top, six generalized scenes provide a rare representation of this sub-culture. In particular, the first scene shows an all-male party, with two men of similar age walking off together hand in hand, watched by a personification of 'Sin'. In the second, they are shown abandoning their families to go off together, watched by 'Sorrow'. The remainder show their arrest, imprisonment and execution in front of Amsterdam's city hall (shown bottom right). The scenes are accompanied by a long poem, describing their actions as 'blacker than the pools of miserable Sodom', with lines such as:

> Tremble sinner! For you shall not escape capital
> punishment …
> Even as your filthy mind trembles at the
> impending pain,
> Nothing can help you, for punishment follows
> the sin.

Ironically, Amsterdam is now one of the most accepting cities for people from the lesbian, gay, bisexual and transgender communities, and the Netherlands was the first country in the world to legalize same-sex marriage. The first marriage took place in 2001 in the same city hall that is shown on the broadsheet.

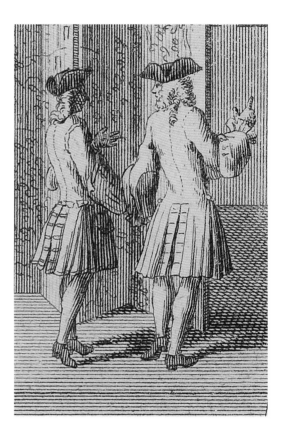

OPPOSITE The moral images at the top of the broadsheet *This-worldly Punishment Represented to Deter all Godless and Damnable Sinners*. Amsterdam, 1730.
Paper, 18.6 x 28.4 cm.

ABOVE Two gentlemen committing the sin of holding hands.

EROTIC VOYEURISM

Traditional Japanese theatre has a convention of transforming sexual identities in performance, as with Shakespeare's plays. In the seventeenth century, women were banned from appearing on the Kabuki stage, and men performed female roles. Near a city's Kabuki theatres, there were teahouses where actors could meet their patrons, and young actors of female roles would sometimes provide sexual services to paying clients. These male-male relationships

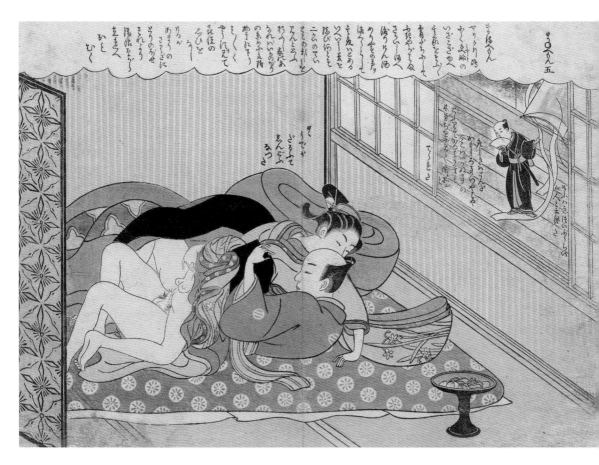

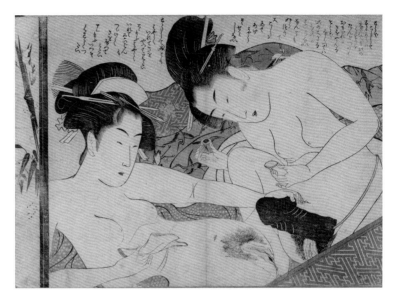

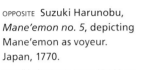 OPPOSITE Suzuki Harunobu, *Mane'emon no. 5*, depicting Mane'emon as voyeur. Japan, 1770.

Woodblock print on paper, 20 x 28 cm.

RIGHT Chōkyōsai Eiri, from *Fumi no kiyogaki*. Two women anointing a sex toy with lubricant. Japan, 1801.

Woodblock print on paper, 25 x 35.9 cm.

were often structured by age, as with the samurai, who made up a significant part of the clientele for this not entirely legal demimonde.

This colour woodblock print from 1770 is one of a series of prints, *Elegant Amorous Mane'emon*, by the artist Suzuki Harunobu (died 1770). They illustrate the adventures of Ukiyonosuke, who is transformed into the tiny Mane'emon ('Bean-man') and who then uses his size to spy on various people making love: his role as a voyeur mirrors that of the viewer of the erotic work of art. Here Mane'emon flies on a kite up to the window of a teahouse to observe a young trainee Kabuki actor in bed with a client. The attractive young actor

strokes himself as his client makes love to him. Mane'emon comments

> Good heavens, the method of having male sex involves some elaborate handiwork.

Such commercial erotic prints were produced from the sixteenth to nineteenth centuries, and could include women making love together: in one album by Chōkyōsi Eiri (worked 1790s– 1801) most of the twelve prints show men with women, but one shows two women together, preparing to use a sex toy. One of the women says 'Hurry up and put it in.'

A CELEBRITY SOLDIER

Even in a hostile world, it is striking how complicated and varied lives could be. Charles-Geneviève-Louis-Auguste-André-Timothée d'Éon de Beaumont, the Chevalier d'Éon (1728–1810), worked as a diplomat and spy for King Louis XV of France, dressing sometimes as a woman and sometimes as a man. He/she claimed that she was born female, and had been brought up as a man to secure the family inheritance. In 1779, she published her memoirs as *The Military, Political and Private Life of Mlle d'Éon*. She ended up living in political exile in England with a state pension from the French court with the official condition that she dress as a woman. She lived as a woman with a widowed friend, Mrs Coles, but when she died in poverty in London in 1810, a post-mortem examination declared that she was anatomically male. Nothing is known of her desires or romantic relationships.

At one point a betting pool about her gender had even been set up in London, and she took to the stage as a female fencer to raise money. Perhaps unsurprisingly, she features in many British satirical prints, such as this one where a fashionably dressed lady incongruously holds a man's sword: on the wall behind her, pictures of two notorious hoaxes (one is a woman giving birth to rabbits) suggest that her claims to be a woman were also fraudulent. But more sympathetic portraits exist, including this print of 1787 (opposite). The only explicit sign of gender ambiguity here is the masculine military cross proudly worn on the breast, and she looks untroubled by any doubts or conflicts about identity.

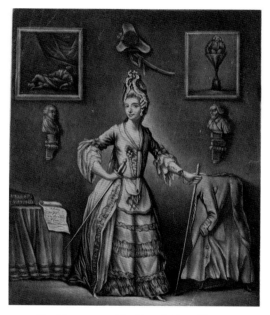

ABOVE *The Discovery or The Female Free-Mason.* Britain, 1771.

Mezzotint print on paper, 31.1 x 25.2 cm.

OPPOSITE Thomas A. E. Chambars, *Mademoiselle La Chevalier d'Éon de Beaumont*, a stipple print from a drawing by Richard Cosway (1742–1821). London, 1787.

Stipple print on paper, 17.3 x 11.2 cm.

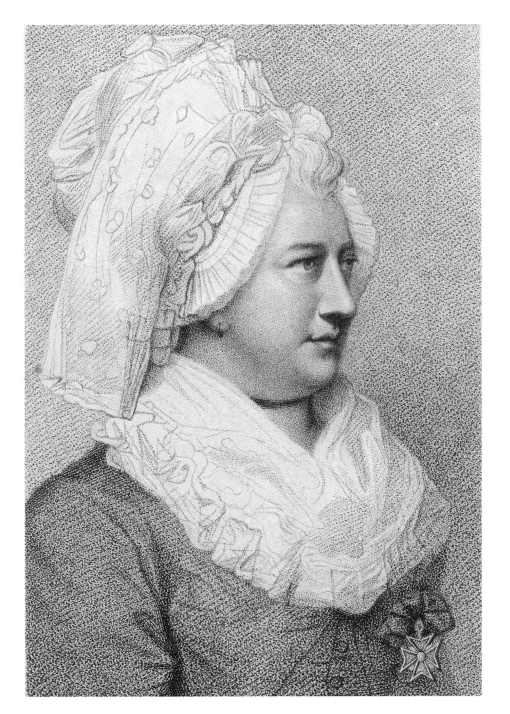

PACIFIC EMBRACES

In the early eighteenth century, European explorers recorded sexual practices between males in the eastern Pacific region. European missionaries and colonial officials in the following centuries strongly discouraged such activities.

In many parts of the eastern Pacific or Polynesia, same-sex acts were tolerated only between a gender-crossing male and a socially accepted man. Polynesian languages have terms such as *mahu* (Tahiti) and *fa'a fafine* (Samoa) that define men who act and dress as women and who, as in many areas of South-East Asia, represent a third gender between man and woman. However, not all man on man sex involved such individuals: in Hawaii, *aikane* were young masculine men who had sex with the king. David Samwell (1751–98), a Welsh surgeon on Captain Cook's ship *The Discovery*, noted in 1779 with some surprise that

> it is an office that is esteemed honourable among them & they have frequently asked us on seeing a handsome young fellow if he was not an [*aikane*] to some of us.

This box from eighteenth-century New Zealand is made of wood and decorated with shell. It is a so-called 'treasure box' that would contain the powerful personal ornaments of a high-ranking Maori person, such as a chief. Every surface (including the underneath) of this prestigious box is covered with designs which show fourteen highly stylized figures, intertwined and linked in various types of sexual union, several showing an embrace between two males.

OPPOSITE, ABOVE This 'treasure box' was designed to be stored, not on the ground, but suspended. New Zealand, late eighteenth century. Wood and shell, H. 9.4 cm; L. 43 cm; D 9.8 cm.

OPPOSITE, BELOW A stylized scene of oral sex on one side of the box.

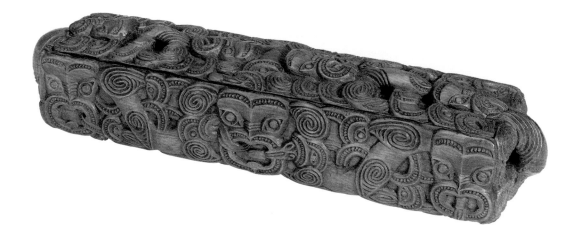

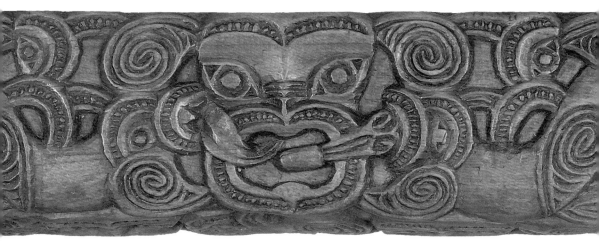

ENGLISH ABROAD

Persecution in Europe affected even establishment figures. One individual whose life was wrecked was the British dilettante, antiquarian, Member of Parliament and close friend of Lord Byron, William John Bankes (1786–1855). In this letter of 1818, the English polymath Thomas Young (1773–1829) writes a message to be forwarded to him while he was in Egypt, asking him to look out for the missing fragments of the Rosetta Stone in order to help with deciphering ancient Egyptian hieroglyphs.

Nothing seems unusual here, but in 1833 Bankes was tried for soliciting a guardsman in a public toilet in London. Bankes was acquitted but retired from public life, managing to maintain his social standing. But then on 30 August 1841, he was again caught with a soldier and was arrested for

that detestable & abominable crime (amongst Christians not to be named) called Buggery ... against the order of nature.

In the absence of any socially approved spaces, public parks after dark offered places for same-sex desire. Court records say that a police officer had followed him and a soldier into Green Park in London one night and found them

both sitting on a Bench near the Clump of Trees close together. I saw the Prisoner's Private parts exposed, his small Clothes being unbuttoned and the Soldier had got hold of the Prisoner's yard [penis].

The soldier ran off and 'made his escape'. Bankes was arrested, and as soon as he was released on bail he fled the country to avoid the court case. He remained in Europe, where attitudes and laws were less severe than in Britain, until his death in Venice in 1855.

OPPOSITE Thomas Young's letter to Bankes' father. London, 10 February 1818.
Paper, 22.7 x 18.4 cm.

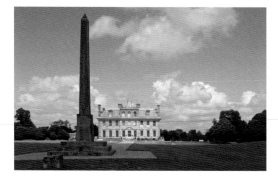

LEFT Bankes' house at Kingston Lacy, Dorset, with an Egyptian obelisk collected on his travels.

Dear Sir   Welbeck Street Tuesday 10 Feb. 1818

                    I send you a few memorandums, which I shall be much obliged
by your forwarding to your son, for the chance of his receiving them before his return to
Egypt, as I doubt not that so enlightened and enterprising a traveller will be as willing
as he is able to assist in promoting the investigation of the hieroglyphical antiquities of
that singular country: and I trust that a few hints of what has already been done will
enable him to effect this purpose, with considerably less labour than might otherwise have
been bestowed on it.
                    1. The great desideratum of all is the recovery of the lost fragments
of the Rosetta stone, which to an Egyptian antiquary would be worth their weight in
diamonds. The part found by the French contains little more than one third of the
inscription in the "sacred characters"; and this portion, imperfect as it is, has afforded an
explanation of above fifty hieroglyphics; a number which would be more than doubled
by the discovery of the remainder. Mr. Salt was empowered by the British government
to expend a liberal sum in digging in the neighbourhood of Fort St. Julien, or otherwise,
in pursuit of this object; but there is reason to fear that it has wholly escaped his memory.
                    2. A duplicate of this stone is described by Dr. Clarke as having been
seen by him in the house occupied by the Institute at Cairo, but in imperfect preservation.
It would be of the utmost importance to have this duplicate brought to England, since the slightest
traces might possibly be rendered intelligible by a careful comparison: and it is indeed hoped that
Mr. Salt has already taken measures for this purpose.
                    3. The inedited inscriptions on the ruins of buildings still existing in Egypt,
and even on unwrought blocks and rocks are far too numerous to be copied by any single
traveller: it becomes therefore of importance to be directed to the most important parts of them:
which are commonly the names of the kings whom they commemorate, and those of the deities
to whom they are dedicated. The names of the deities are generally distinguished by a
hatchet or a sitting figure which follows them; those of the kings universally by an oval
ring which surrounds them, preceded by a reed and a bee: and frequently followed by a
goose and a circle, and then a second name, which is that of the father.
                    4. The inscriptions almost universally relate to the figures over or
before which they are placed; and they are always read from the front to the rear of the figures;
but from right to left, or from left to right, almost indifferently.

                                    Specimens

A God	...	King	...	One	...	Ptolemy	...
A Goddess		Son		Two		Berenice	
Phthah, or Vulcan		Life		Ten		Amenophis or Memnon	
Phre, or the Sun		Eternity		C		Mestphres	
Thoth, or Hermes		Immortal		M		Rammis, or Seneutes	
Osiris		Day		A plural		Soter	
Isis		Month		Of, or to		Epiphanes	
Aroeris, or Apollo		Year		Upon		Eucharistus	
Nephthe, or Aphrodite		Temple		And		Philometor, or possibly Philopater	

H. Bankes Esq.   I am, dear Sir, your faithful and obedient servant Thomas Young

Katsushika Hokusai, painting of a 'lovely form' watching the spring. Japan, 1840.

Painted silk, 80.4 x 32.7 cm.

SPRING IN JAPAN

Beyond Christian Europe, things were different. This beautifully detailed and elegantly restrained painting on a silk scroll is by the famous artist Katsushika Hokusai (1760–1849), and was probably commissioned by a patron. It shows a youth wearing a sword and dressed in a feminine-looking blue kimono with long, flowing sleeves decorated with white cherry blossom. He sits on a bench and is apparently on an outing to admire the cherry trees in spring. A poem is written on the painting in Chinese-style couplets by someone who calls himself 'your servant'. It is addressed to 'young Sessen' who must be the young man who is clearly much admired by the (male) speaker:

> Spring breezes and spring rains assail his
>   lovely form.
> Even the dew weighs heavily on branches of
>   the evanescent cherry.
> Why does he seem so lost in thought, like a
>   beautiful woman,
> As he rests there on the bench, overcome
>   with waves of tears?

The painting and poem convey a sense not only of the young man's beauty but also an atmosphere of sophisticated romance and delicate passion. This scene is a world away from William Bankes' search for rough trade on the bench in the bushes of Green Park, London. The picture and poem say it all.

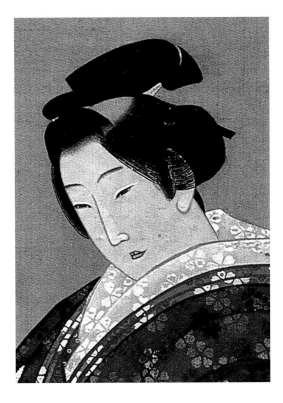

The face of the 'beautiful one'.

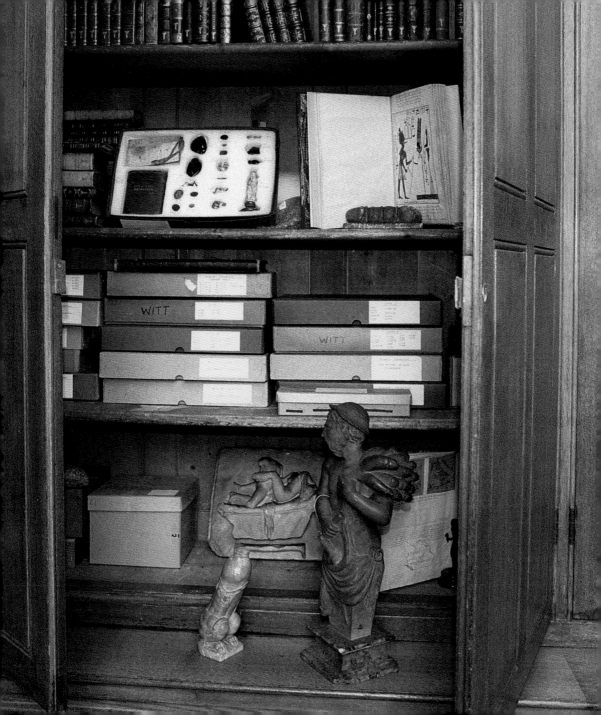

FROM SECRET TO SCIENCE

The Roman cities of Pompeii and Herculaneum were discovered in the eighteenth century and startled people with their explicit depictions of sex. Soon the Italian authorities decided to keep such 'obscene' items apart in the museum at Naples, and the same thing was done in the British Museum from the 1830s.

Later in 1865, the Museum established its own 'Secretum' (secret museum) after the donation of a collection of hundreds of phallic objects by George Witt (1804–69); one of these was the Greek vase on page 46. Witt had made his fortune in Australia and then returned to London and collected antiquities, including these 'Symbols of the early Worship of Mankind'. Access to view such items was limited to prevent vulnerable members of society (women, children and the lower classes) from being corrupted by such obscenities; this arrangement also allowed gentlemen with special permission to see them all conveniently grouped together.

The Secretum – which no longer exists – shows the ways in which representations of sex in general have been controlled. But it also shows how people were beginning to study human sexuality across cultures in a scientific manner, and it is part of a tradition that led to the work of the German physician and sexologist Magnus Hirschfeld (1868–1935). Around the same period as the Secretum was founded, the term 'homosexuality' was first coined in Germany, and it was first used in English in 1891. Desire was now medicalized into black and white categories of 'homo-' and 'heterosexual', with 'homosexuals' as a distinct type of person. Hirschfeld's hope was that scientific study would increase understanding and tolerance of the phenomenon.

OPPOSITE A reconstruction of how the Secretum might have appeared to visitors.

RIGHT Two ancient Egyptian phallic amulets from the Secretum, from around the fourth century BC or later.
Glazed composition, H. 4 cm.

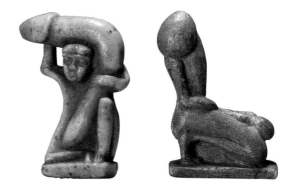

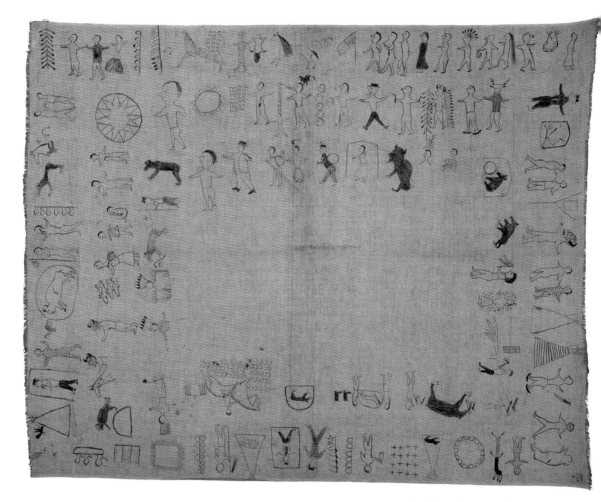

A 'Winter Count', relating over a century of history. Earlier examples were on hide, but this one is a later example on muslin. North America, 1891.

Muslin, L. 122 cm; W. 88 cm.

ONE YEAR IN NORTH AMERICA

Among some tribes of the North American plains, 'Winter Counts' were kept as historical records. Each year (counted from winter to winter) was known by a memorable event, which was represented by an image on these records. This is one of many surviving versions of a Sioux 'count' that sometimes included different events for each year, and it shows the winters of 1785/6 to 1901/2 in a sequence of 119 images. Here, the year 1891 includes an image representing the suicide of a *winkte* (a word in the Dakota language meaning literally 'wants to be a woman'). This was a category of males whose occupations and social roles were those of women. From other 'Winter Counts' and indigenous comments we learn that the winter of one earlier year was called 'Grass killed himself' after a *winkte* who 'had troubles with his folks and hanged himself'.

Among many Native American tribes, such individuals were considered to be endowed with special spiritual powers because they bridged gender differences. Among the Dakota Sioux Indians, there were at any given time up to ten (recorded) individuals belonging to this class of people in the same tribe. After the arrival of Anglo-Americans and the institution of reservations in the late nineteenth century, the practice of cross-dressing by such individuals was repressed. Today a revival of this tradition is flourishing among younger generations of lesbian, gay, bisexual and transgender Native Americans who see these figures as their forebears and a traditional source of inspiration with which to revive past customs.

A figure dressed as a woman hangs himself, from the winter of 1891.

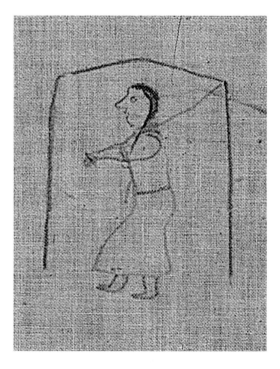

DESIRE IN THE MUSEUM

For many university-educated people in nineteenth-century Europe, ancient Greece offered images of a world where same-sex desire ('Greek love') was not incompatible with cultural ideals, and where it was not 'abnormal'. Classical statuary let people view the naked human form in a respectable way, allowing men to gaze at men, which was otherwise unacceptable. As in ancient Athens, these statues had an erotic charge: one male visitor to a museum at this period recorded that 'I revelled in the sight of pictures and statues of male form and could not keep from kissing [them]'. This photograph (opposite) shows a statue of an athlete in the galleries of the British Museum; it was taken in 1857 by Roger Fenton (1819–69).

Mediterranean and Indian cultures offered a sense of freedom from English respectability for the novelist E. M. Forster (1879–1970). His own sexuality informed all his works, but was embodied most openly in his novel *Maurice*, which was finished in 1914 but not published until after his death. The book tells of the growing self-awareness of a Cambridge graduate who eventually finds love with a gamekeeper, and the turning point takes place in the classical galleries of the British Museum, on an evening when 'the great building suggested a tomb, miraculously illuminated

by the spirits of the dead'. Here the two men quarrel and reach an understanding of love, as rough trade turns into romance and an enduring relationship. Forster himself found happiness with a married policeman.

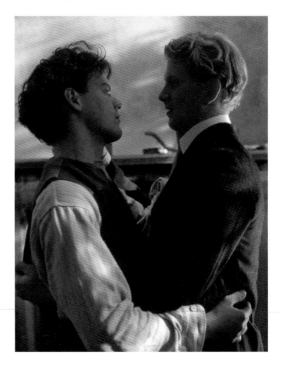

The Forsterian triumph of love: Maurice Hall and the gamekeeper Alec Scudder embrace at the end of the film *Maurice* by Merchant Ivory Productions, starring James Wilby and Rupert Graves, 1987.

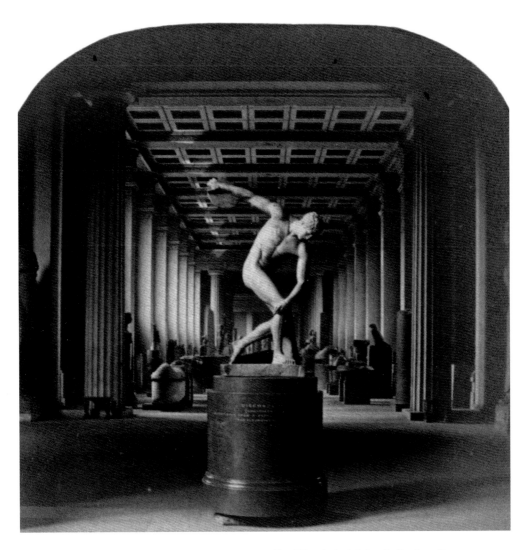

The 'Discobolus' statue in the Egyptian
sculpture gallery of the British Museum in 1857.
The statue is a Roman copy of a lost Greek
original and was found in Hadrian's villa at Tivoli.

Photographic print on paper, 7.6 x 7.1 cm.

OUT IN AFRICA

In many African cultures, as in many other societies, gender and gendered roles are culturally reproduced and fixed through rituals, including initiation ceremonies. The N'domo initiation ceremony of the Bamana people from Mali, for example, has male masks, female masks and androgynous masks: the gender is indicated by the number of horns (masks with seven horns represent androgyny). The ungendered status of uninitiated children relates them to mythical ancestors, who are often represented as androgynous figures or a pair made up of a male and a female figure, such as those carved by the Dogon of Mali.

Little is known about this small steatite figure, collected by Major H. F. Maxsted from Sierra Leone sometime before 1920, but it appears to be hermaphrodite, and may represent an ancestor of the Mende people. It is, however, hard to read the visual conventions of another culture, and the apparently female breasts might be male pectoral muscles and nipples.

Anthropological and historical evidence shows that same-sex sexual practices and a variety of gender configurations were known in Africa before the arrival of Europeans. These practices and beliefs were largely prohibited by colonial administrators, and have often been forgotten, creating the impression that such things never existed on this continent. Partly as a result of this history and the introduction of Christianity, 'homosexuality' is now illegal in many African countries. Civil rights for people of colour have often run parallel to rights for lesbian, gay, bisexual and transgender people, and in 2012 Archbishop Tutu commented

> I have no doubt that in the future, the laws that criminalise so many forms of love and human commitment will look the way the apartheid laws do to us now – so obviously wrong.

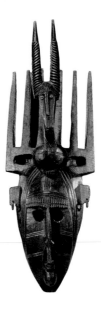

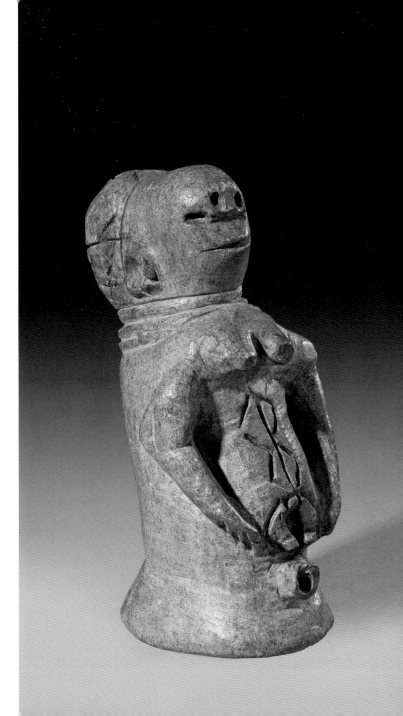

RIGHT A small stone figure from Sierra Leone, created some time before 1920.

Steatite, H. 15 cm; W. 6.5 cm.

OPPOSITE A female N'domo initiation mask: the gender is indicated by the number of horns (here six). Mali, early twentieth century.

Wood, H. 56 cm.

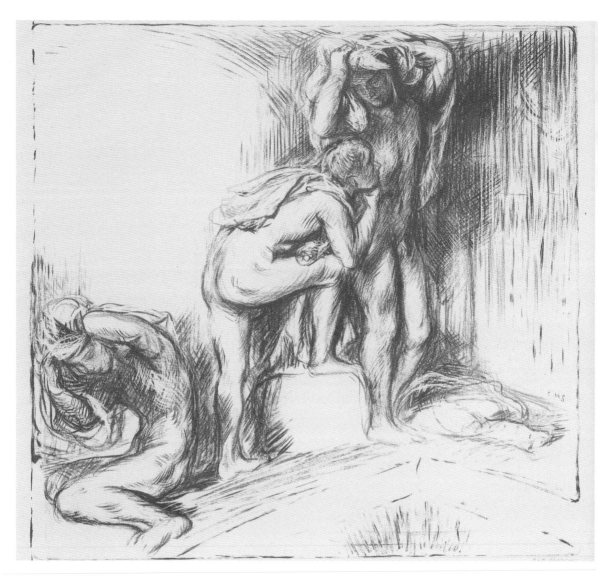

Charles Shannon, *The Bath.*
London, 1905.

Lithograph on paper, 30 x 30.6 cm.

AESTHETIC AND OTHER MOVEMENTS

In 1895, the infamous trial of the writer and aesthete Oscar Wilde (1854–1900) showed how great public hostility could be to anyone with 'abnormal' sexual tastes. Intense discretion was necessary. At the same time, there were political movements towards legal reform, as in the writings of the inspirational socialist Edward Carpenter (1844–1929), who lived openly with his male partner. But few lives could be lived so publicly, and many people could not admit such things even to themselves.

The Aesthetic movement, with its emphasis on art for art's sake, offered a challenge to conventional ideas of English masculinity and bourgeois morality. Charles Ricketts (1866–1931) met Charles Shannon (1863–1937) on his sixteenth birthday at the City and Guilds Art School in Kennington. They lived together for fifty years, in a working partnership as painters, book- and theatre-designers and sculptors, devoting their lives entirely to art. They were friends of Oscar Wilde, and illustrated his works. It is now impossible to know the exact nature of Ricketts and Shannon's loving relationship, which was probably largely, if not entirely, sexless. Shannon was certainly attracted to women, although this sensuous lithograph of 1905,

The Bath, suggests that he could also be responsive to male beauty. Rickett's devotion, however, makes it clear that he loved mainly men, although his erotic feelings were apparently never voiced directly even to himself. In 1906, he noted in his own diary 'I have ... been frightened by the question, "What should I do if Shannon got married?"'. But while Shannon sometimes wanted to, he never did.

Charles Shannon, *Portrait of the Artist*. London, 1905.

Lithograph on paper, 30 x 30.6 cm.

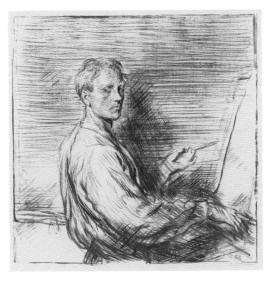

EXPRESSIONIST CERAMICS

Hedwig Marquardt (1884–1969) and Augusta Kaiser (1895–1932) were ceramicists in the period of German Expressionism and Art Deco, and their careers exemplify the difficulties women artists faced in a male-dominated profession in the early twentieth century, even when women's rights were changing. Hedwig Marquardt was trained as

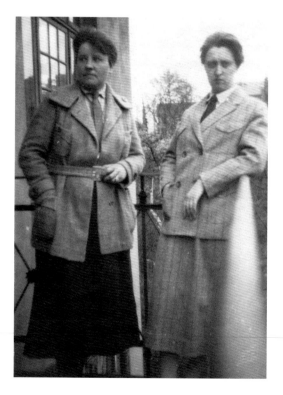

a painter but had to turn to pottery to make a living, and she met Augusta Kaiser – known as Gust – in May 1922, while working for a ceramic manufacturer. They became friends and then life partners: 'only love is here – with Hedwig + Gust'. They worked together for the newly founded Kieler Kunst-Keramik firm in Kiel, and left to try to live as independent artists and ceramicists, but in 1927 Marquardt took a teaching post in Hannover. Kaiser died young from illness in 1932, and Marquardt later lived with the artist Charlotte Boltze (1881–1959).

These three glazed earthenware figures from Kieler Kunst-Keramik were designed by Augusta Kaiser around 1924–5. They are inspired by classical sculpture, and are very Michelangelesque. While the cream glazing on a red body is typical of the period, this modelling is much more distinctive. Two of these small domestic pieces show a woman's body represented by a woman artist, and they were owned by Hedwig Marquardt and kept by her after Augusta Kaiser's death. On her own death in 1969, they were bequeathed to her niece Christel Marsh, and were given to the Museum in memory of Mrs Marsh. All too often, such lives and stories slip out of history and are forgotten.

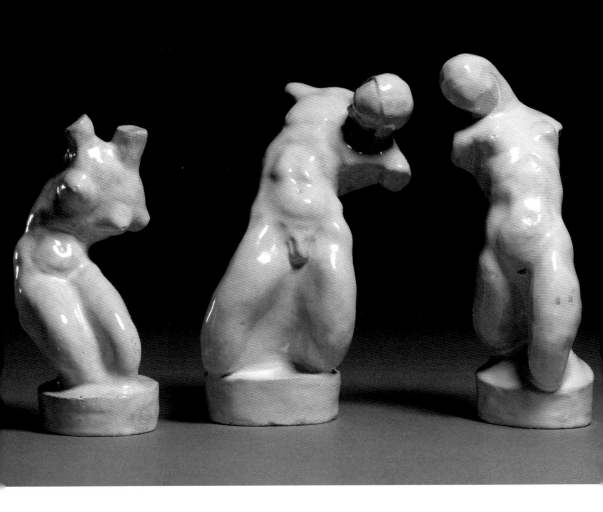

ABOVE Three figurines by Augusta
Kaiser. Kiel, Germany, c. 1924–5.

Glazed earthenware, H. (male figurine) 15.5 cm.

OPPOSITE Hedwig Marquardt and
Augusta Kaiser in Kiel in 1925
(Kaiser is on the right).

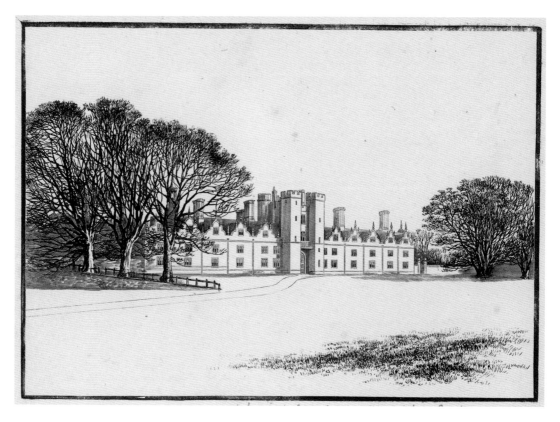

A HISTORICAL FACADE

This wood-engraving of the great Tudor house of Knole in Kent shows a rather conventional image of one of the 'Seats of the Noblemen and Gentlemen of Great Britain and Ireland' from a series printed by Benjamin Fawcett (1808–93). About the same time that the view was printed,

Virginia Woolf (1882–1941) was born, and she would provide another view of this house in her novel *Orlando: A Biography*, published in 1928. This book was inspired by her affair with the 'bisexual' Vita Sackville-West (1892–1962), the only child of the aristocratic family

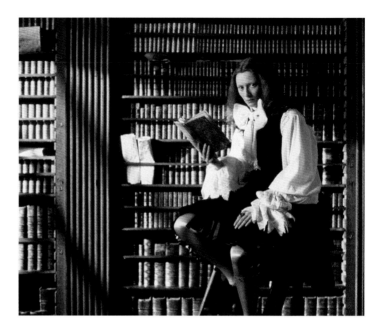

OPPOSITE Benjamin Fawcett, *Knole House*. A view of the house seen from the park. Britain, *c.* 1880.

Wood-engraving on paper, 13.8 x 19.6 cm.

RIGHT The hero(ine) surrounded by history, as portrayed by Tilda Swinton in the 1992 film *Orlando*, directed by Sally Potter.

who owned the house, which Vita could not inherit because she was a woman. She was happily married to the 'bisexual' diplomat Harold Nicholson, and both had affairs with members of their own sex.

Woolf's novel offers a vision of the un-inheritable house for her lover, and it presents a woman's view of history through a subversive mock-biography of an Elizabethan nobleman. Orlando lives across centuries, travels, changes sex, and pursues love, life and literature. At the heart of the book is the old house, at once unchanging and constantly changing with passing history, just like its owner:

There it lay in the early sunshine of spring. It looked a town rather than a house ... built, Orlando thought, by workmen whose names are unknown. Here have lived, for more centuries than I can count, the obscure generations of my own obscure family ... Never had the house looked more noble and humane.

Woolf's extraordinarily funny and profound vision reminds us that not every history has to take a conventional viewpoint.

LOVES ANCIENT AND MODERN

This etching of two men in bed is by the British artist David Hockney (born 1937). It illustrates a poem by the great Greek poet C. P. Cavafy (1863–1933), entitled 'In the Dull Village', describing a young man in a village dreaming of love. Hockney discovered Cavafy's poems in his local library as a student in the north of England, when the volume was considered too erotic to be on the open shelves. He was later commissioned to produce a set of illustrations to the poems. The prints were made in the late 1960s when attitudes towards same-sex desire were increasingly liberal, and when such desire could again be acknowledged and celebrated. Hockney, who now lives with his partner in Bridlington, produced openly gay paintings from the start of the 1960s.

C. P. Cavafy lived in the cosmopolitan Egyptian city of Alexandria, and his subtle and ironic poems often evoked the world of the Hellenistic and Byzantine Mediterranean with sensuous re-creations of the ancient city. Some of them feature erotic desire between men in both modern and ancient settings:

> But as soon as he saw his friend come in –
> Fatigue, boredom and ill thoughts vanished
> at once …

> And once they'd run out of expensive drinks,
> And since, by then, it was nearing four o'clock,
> They abandoned themselves blissfully to love.

Cavafy was among the earliest modern authors to write openly about same-sex love, although during his lifetime most of his poems were only privately printed and circulated.

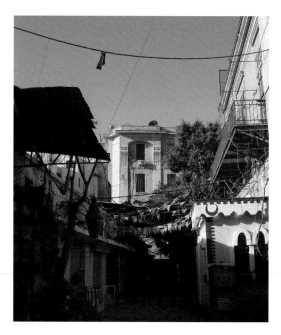

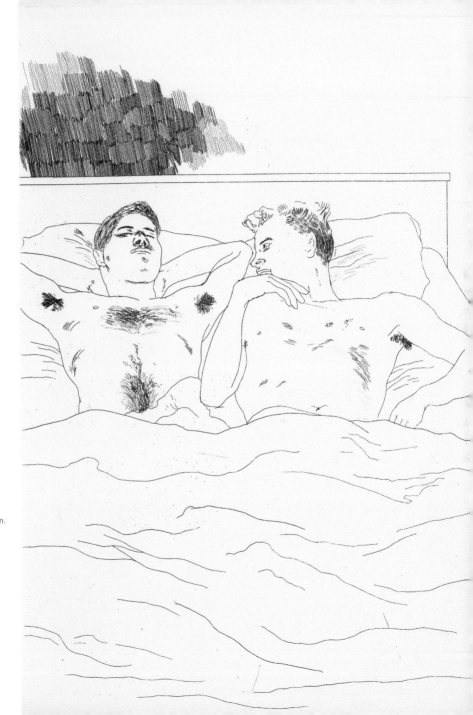

RIGHT David Hockney,
In the Dull Village.
Britain, 1966–7.

Etching on paper, 35 x 22.5 cm.

OPPOSITE Cavafy's
second floor flat on
the rue Lepsius,
Alexandria, where
many of his poems
were written, now a
museum to the poet.

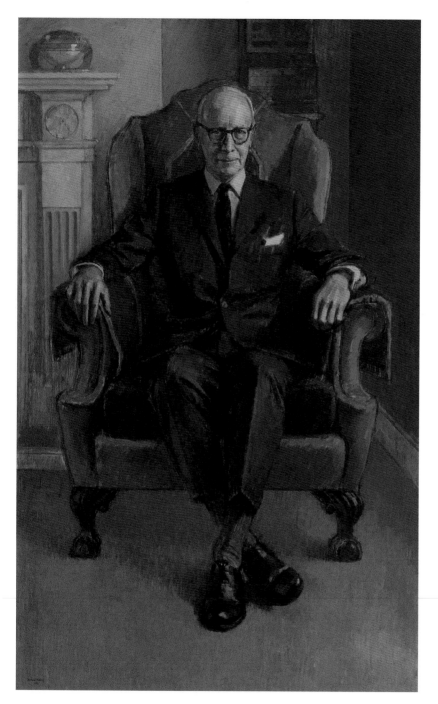

A 'straight ally': John Wolfenden as Museum director. London, 1974.

Oil on canvas, 117.5 x 74 cm.

TOWARDS EQUALITY

Although attitudes were changing, the laws in many countries did not. In 1954, a government committee was set up in Britain to review laws on 'homosexual offences'. It was chaired by John Wolfenden (1906–85), and in 1957 it recommended the decriminalization of 'homosexual behaviour between consenting adults in private'. Wolfenden's was an impartial legal report, although it later turned out that his son was 'homosexual'.

The Conservative government of the period did not act on Wolfenden's recommendations, and organizations continued to press for reform. No public figure could be openly 'homosexual' without running the risk of prosecution, and when 'homosexuals' did appear in the media, it was often as comic camp stereotypes. While these caricatures put many people off from identifying as gay, even this visibility helped change public opinion. In 1967, love-making between two men (in private and over the age of twenty-one) was decriminalized in Britain, although men could still be arrested for kissing in public places.

Wolfenden was later a director of the British Museum from 1969 to 1973. This portrait is by Michael Noakes (born 1933). It was painted in 1974 and is contemporary with the first Gay Pride marches in London, which

Wolfenden's report had ultimately enabled. Such pressure on successive British governments ensured that the age of consent was made equal for 'homosexual' (including lesbian) and 'heterosexual' couples in 2000. However, full equal rights are still not yet achieved in many countries of the world, and being lesbian, gay, bisexual or transgender remains a crime in some, often as a legacy of earlier British legislation.

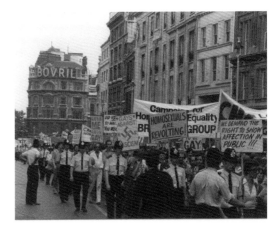

The first London Gay Pride
march on 1 July 1972.

PROTESTS AND RIGHTS

These badges from protest rallies were worn both by protesters and also by others as signs of their support for lesbian and gay rights. They represent four decades and a wide range of issues: some are specific, such as the threatened closure of a gay bookshop, while some are general. Some are serious, and some wittily caricature stereotypes about gay identity, such as the assumption that if you are a lesbian, you must own a cat, as in the badge by the cartoonist Kate Charlesworth.

Several of these designs include the pink triangle, a symbol with a dark history. The Nazi regime in Germany persecuted and killed millions of citizens whom they considered undesirable. These were predominantly Jews but also included trade unionists, communists, gypsies, physically disabled people and 'homosexuals'. An estimated hundred thousand 'homosexual' men were arrested, and those who were sent to concentration camps were made to wear the pink triangle. After the camps were liberated, some were re-imprisoned because 'homosexuality' remained illegal in Germany, and it was only in the 1980s that these forgotten victims began to be acknowledged officially. Campaigning organizations reclaimed the triangle as a badge of gay pride, inverting it, and it was widely used by the 1970s.

Such badges are still being produced, and people continue to fight for lesbian, gay, bisexual and transgender rights to be fully recognized. As the campaigner Peter Tatchell comments:

the only liberation struggle worth fighting is a struggle inspired by love. Love is the beginning, middle and end of liberation. Without love, there can be no liberation worthy of the name.

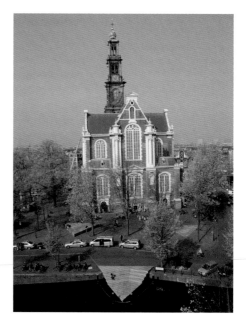

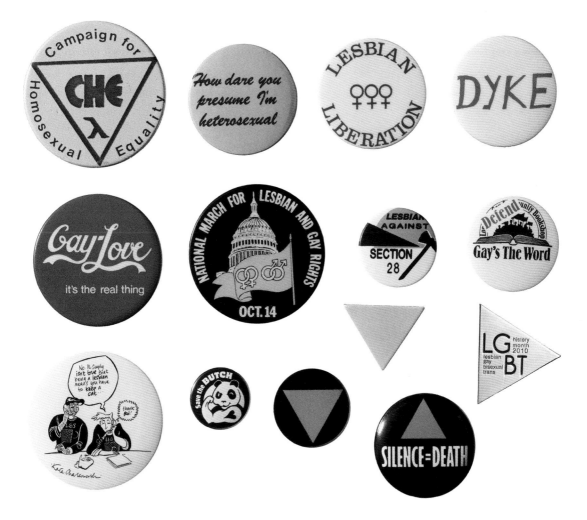

OPPOSITE The pink triangle is often included in the memorials to gay victims of the Second World War, as in the 'Homomonument' in Amsterdam, opened in 1987.

ABOVE British and American badges from the 1970s onwards.

Plastic, paper and metal, H. ('LGBT History Month 2010' badge) 3.5 cm; W. 4 cm.

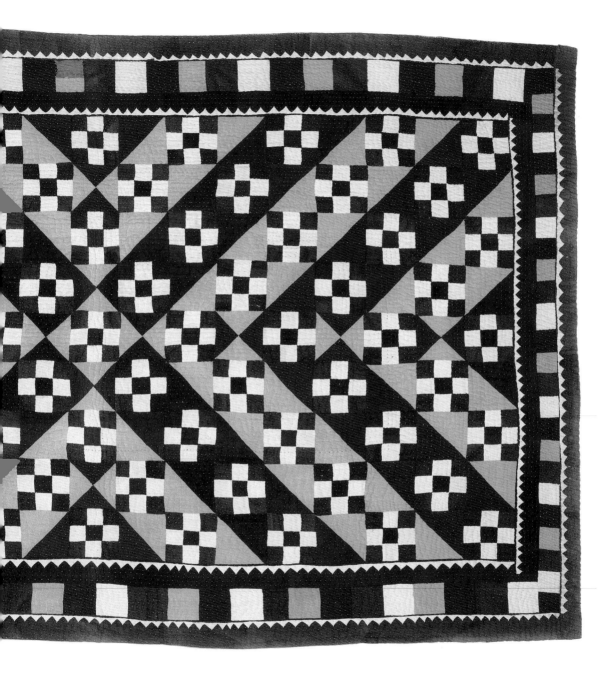

The fabric of an unrecorded
history. Pakistan, 1980s.

Cotton, L. 217 cm; W. 137 cm.

A QUILT

Histories are multiple and often hard to detect.
Protesters make themselves visible and demand
a voice, but many communities do not have
such options. This cotton quilt, decorated with
appliqué, was bought in Karachi in Pakistan
by the textile expert John Gillow, and acquired
by the British Museum in 1985. Although
Gillow was told at the time that it was made
by, or for, itinerant transvestites (*hijra*s), he
was not certain that this was necessarily true.

*Hijra*s are men who sometimes have
undergone genital modifications and who
usually live together in communities as women,
earning money through dancing and singing
at weddings, and sometimes by prostitution.
They are often devotees of a mother goddess.
The *hijra*s are one of the few exceptions to the
strict gender roles that are considered
acceptable in Indian society, and popular
culture has often tended to merge the
'homosexual' man with the *hijra*s, as if not
fully acknowledging that a gay man can be a
man in mainstream society. Sometimes, people
may seek profit or entertainment – or both –
by playing on outsiders' prurient interest in
this culture, and so the story about the quilt
might not be true. Even if it is a fiction, it tells
us something about attitudes to the *hijra*s.

But without the anecdotal account from its
acquisition, this quilt would remain simply a
textile. And even with the anecdote, the history
of its maker's life remains a blank. For all the
lesbian, gay, bisexual and transgender people
we can name in history, we must consider how
many thousands of others are unrecorded,
unacknowledged and unremembered.

REMEMBERING THE DEAD

In 1981 a new disease was identified, which was diagnosed first in sexually active gay men. In many countries, fear of this initially untreatable disease produced a backlash against the sexual freedom of the preceding decades. Treatments for HIV/AIDS have now been developed and medical research continues, ensuring that a diagnosis need not be a death sentence.

This is a reproduction of a memorial quilt that was made in 2002 for the British Museum by Native American artist Christopher Gomora; he made the original for the Native American AIDS Project in San Francisco, a city famous for its modern gay community. It was intended as a wall hanging to commemorate those who had died of AIDS, and is made from a single tanned deerskin. It is inspired by traditional robes used to immortalize a warrior's actions, and represents the bravery of the people who have succumbed to the disease. Appliqué beadwork creates a looped red ribbon, the symbol adopted by AIDS awareness campaigns, combined with a Native American medicine wheel (a protective symbol of the interconnectedness of creation), from which hang four eagle feathers. The seven turkey feathers along the bottom hem are chosen to represent the seven directions: north, east, south, west, above, below and the centre.

This quilt also makes reference to the Memorial Quilts Project, which organizes annual displays of commemorative quilts and blankets on the Washington Mall in Washington DC, recording the names of loved ones who have died. Unlike the original quilt, this reproduction does not display the names of the dead, at the request of those involved in its making. It represents unnamed histories, loves and losses.

A Native American memorial hanging. San Francisco, 2002.

Deer skin, cotton and feathers,
L. 130 cm; W. 103 cm.

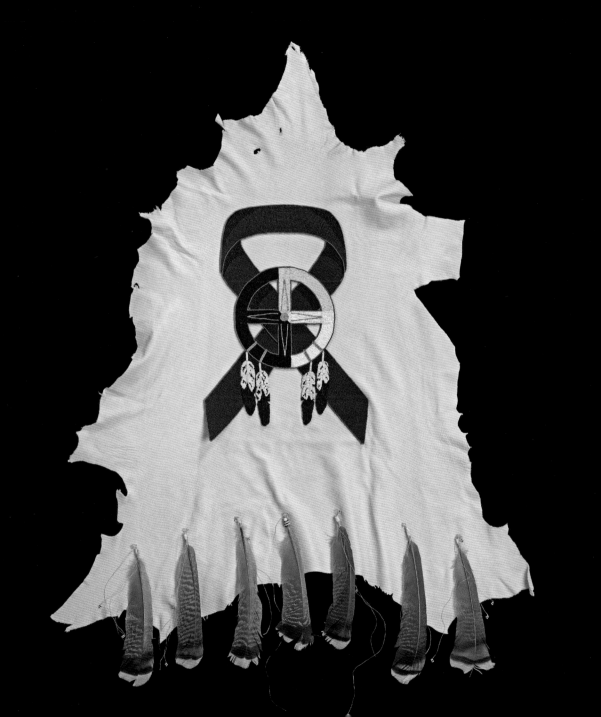

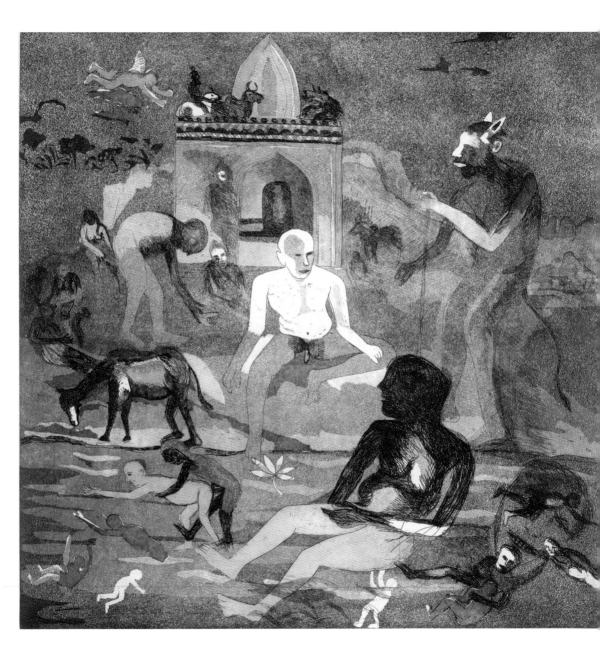

INDIAN LOVES

The Indian artist, Bhupen Khakhar (1934–2003), said that when he was young he 'was very much ashamed of my sexuality. I never wanted it to be known I was gay'. He came out publicly in his fifties despite the fact that 'homosexual' relations remained illegal in India throughout his life: they were criminalized by British colonial laws in 1861 and were decriminalized only in 2009.

Khakhar was a self-taught artist, drawing on a wide range of historical influences, both Indian and European. Almost everything he produced was suffused with an interest in depicting the human body, in keeping with the figurative traditions of Indian art. Rather than physical beauty, however, he was more concerned with 'other aspects, like warmth, pity, vulnerability, touch ...'. It was not immediately obvious to art critics or collectors that he was often depicting his older lover. His work after 1980 became much more explicit, although it maintained its interest in the ordinary, and he became one of India's best known artists internationally.

This intaglio print from 1993 entitled *In the River Jamuna* shows a small riverside shrine, with a *lingam* (phallus) representing the god Shiva, surrounded by figures. Among the smaller figures in the river are men making love. This complex dream-like scene involves images from religious and erotic iconography, and there are also autobiographical elements: the dark figure in the foreground is probably the artist, while the paler figure is probably his lover. The river seems to exist, in the words of one critic, as 'another world of floating free-love'.

OPPOSITE Bhupen Khakhar,
In the River Jamuna. India, 1993.
Intaglio print on paper, 49 x 49 cm.

BELOW Two lovers in the river.

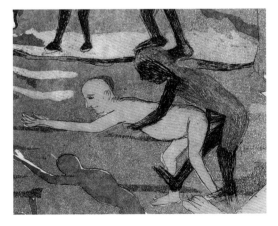

David McDiarmid, *The Family Tree Stops Here Darling*, from the *Rainbow Aphorisms* series. Australia, 1994.

Computer-generated laserprint on paper, 25.8 x 19.5 cm.

THE RAINBOW WORLD

The slow changes in laws and attitudes have often made it difficult for lesbian, gay, bisexual and transgender contributions to society to be recognized. The Nobel-prize winning Australian writer Patrick White (1912–90) met his partner Manoly Lascaris (1912–2003) in Alexandria during the Second World War and lived with him for more than forty years in Australia, but he only wrote publicly about their relationship in the 1980s.

David McDiarmid (1952–95) was a leading Australian artist, DJ and queer political activist. After he was diagnosed HIV-positive in 1987, he devoted himself to producing art to increase awareness of the epidemic and to empower those who were HIV-infected. In 1988–9 he was artistic director of the Sydney Mardi Gras, which began as an annual gay rights march in 1978, and is now a vibrant celebration of gay and lesbian culture which retains its political edge. In this print of 1994, from a series of *Rainbow Aphorisms*, he uses wit and irony to prompt the viewer into some awareness of a different perspective. All allude to the Rainbow Flag, a symbol of gay pride that was first displayed at the Gay Freedom Day Parade in San Francisco in 1978. The rainbow motif is now a worldwide symbol, often replacing the older pink triangle.

The aphorism, printed in the style of a tabloid headline, suggests a camp defiance of the usual social concerns about producing a family: if a child comes out as gay, there's an end to the family tree. 'Gay' can remain celebratory, witty and frivolous about serious things, even in the face of death and oppression.

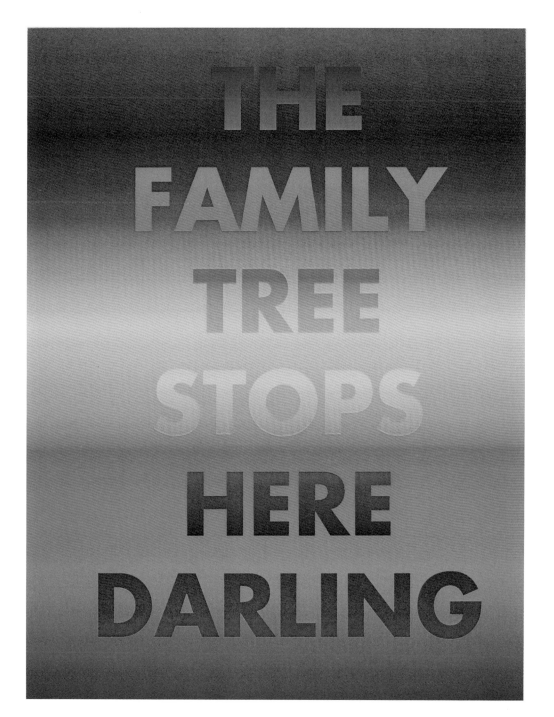

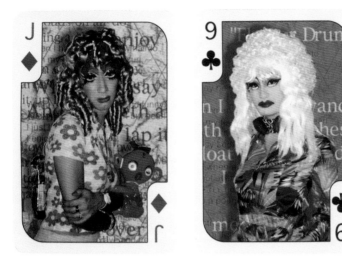

Two queenly cards from the *Drag Queen Deck*.

PLAYING WITH TRADITION

This pack of playing cards shows photographs of drag queens from across Japan. It is not a commercial pack, but a limited edition produced by the artist Ōtsuka Takashi (born 1948). Ōtsuka is a leading figure in Japan's modern gay culture, a bar-owner and activist. Each card shows a different individual, creating a sense of a large community. The text that forms the backdrop to some of the portraits is taken from 'I Enjoy Being a Girl', a song from the Rodgers and Hammerstein musical, *Flower Drum Song* (1958), set in San Francisco's Chinatown. The pack recalls the theatrical traditions of classical Japanese culture, but to witty effect. Despite the long tradition of same-sex love in Japanese high culture, some people in the lesbian, gay, bisexual and transgender communities feel that it is not yet always easy for their lives to be openly recognized, respected or celebrated.

The pack was donated to the museum with the instruction that it should be stored 'with the queens on top'.

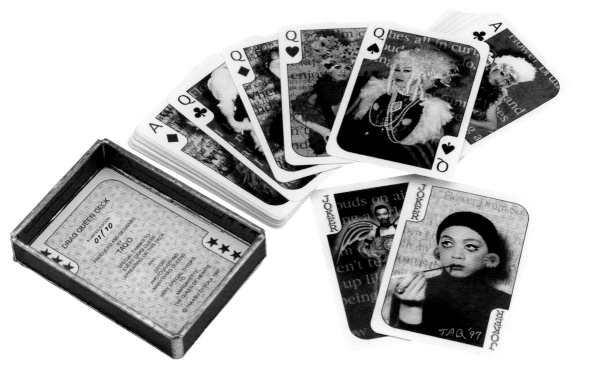

Ōtsuka Takashi, *Drag Queen Deck.*
Tokyo, 1997.

Digital photography on paper, 10.5 x 7.4 cm.

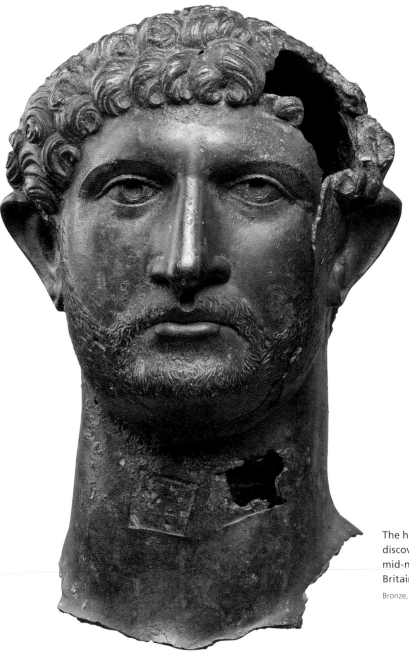

The head from a statue of Hadrian
discovered in the Thames in the
mid-nineteenth century.
Britain, c. 122 BC.

Bronze, H. 43 cm.

TOWARDS A MODERN VIEW

History of course does not stop, and we are all parts of a continually changing reality. So the best final object to include in this brief survey is simply ourselves, as readers or museum visitors who are looking at earlier generations: we too are fragments of this ongoing history. We are not only shaped by this process, but we actively shape it by our own attitudes and actions, no matter whom and how we happen to love.

Now, we can look into the face of a bronze statue of Hadrian in the British Museum. In it, we can see a culture that is partly very different from our own, and partly very familiar. But how can we imagine the inner world, the ideas and feelings that shaped the emperor's expression? How did he love, and how was he loved? As emperor, Hadrian had an unusual liberty to shape his own life. Now, more people have freedom to live their lives as they want to, even though human culture is conventional, and we all live by stereotypes. In terms of sexuality, these stereotypes and labels are often restrictive, but they are now at least quite varied. Perhaps 'lesbian', 'gay', 'LGBT' can now mean many things, from sex to domesticity, and can be regarded as no more and no less 'normal' than anything else. Something that is distinctive but also part of everyday life, individual but part of a culture – exactly like each one of us.

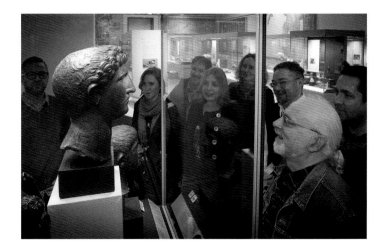

Visitors in the British Museum looking at Hadrian in 2012. All the visitors were happy to appear in this book, regardless of their sexualities. No heterosexuals were harmed in taking this picture.

EPILOGUE:
(RE)-WRITING HISTORIES

All too often, written history is monolithic and not multiple, and it quietly suppresses aspects of life that are not considered 'normal' by the governing culture. But this need not be so: other views are possible.

During a childhood stay in London in 1914–15, the French writer Marguerite Yourcenar (1903–87) saw the bronze head of the emperor Hadrian in the British Museum, and she regarded this visit as contributing to the birth of her historical imagination. She later wrote a re-creation of the emperor's life, including his love for Antinous (see pp. 54–5), in her famous novel *Mémoires d'Hadrien* (1951). This coolly classical, intensely poetic reconstruction of his personality is in many ways also an intensely 'queer' work. At one point in the novel, Hadrian is mourning the drowned Antinous while the imperial entourage is in Luxor, and he visits a famous colossal statue of an ancient pharaoh, which was a tourist site because it seemed to sing at dawn. Instead of leaving yet another official inscription, he simply carves his name in Greek, a single word as

> a life sum (of which the innumerable elements would never be known), a mere mark left by a man wholly lost in that succession of centuries.

A manuscript page of phrases in Greek and Latin copied by Marguerite Yourcenar around 1950, from historical sources connected with her *Memoirs of Hadrian*.

Paper, 28 x 25.6 cm.

Yourcenar based this episode on the official inscriptions on the statue's feet and ankles recording the visit of the imperial entourage. But there are none with just his name in Greek, 'Adriano'. Here the immensely scholarly Yourcenar apparently re-wrote the historical evidence, making her emperor subvert

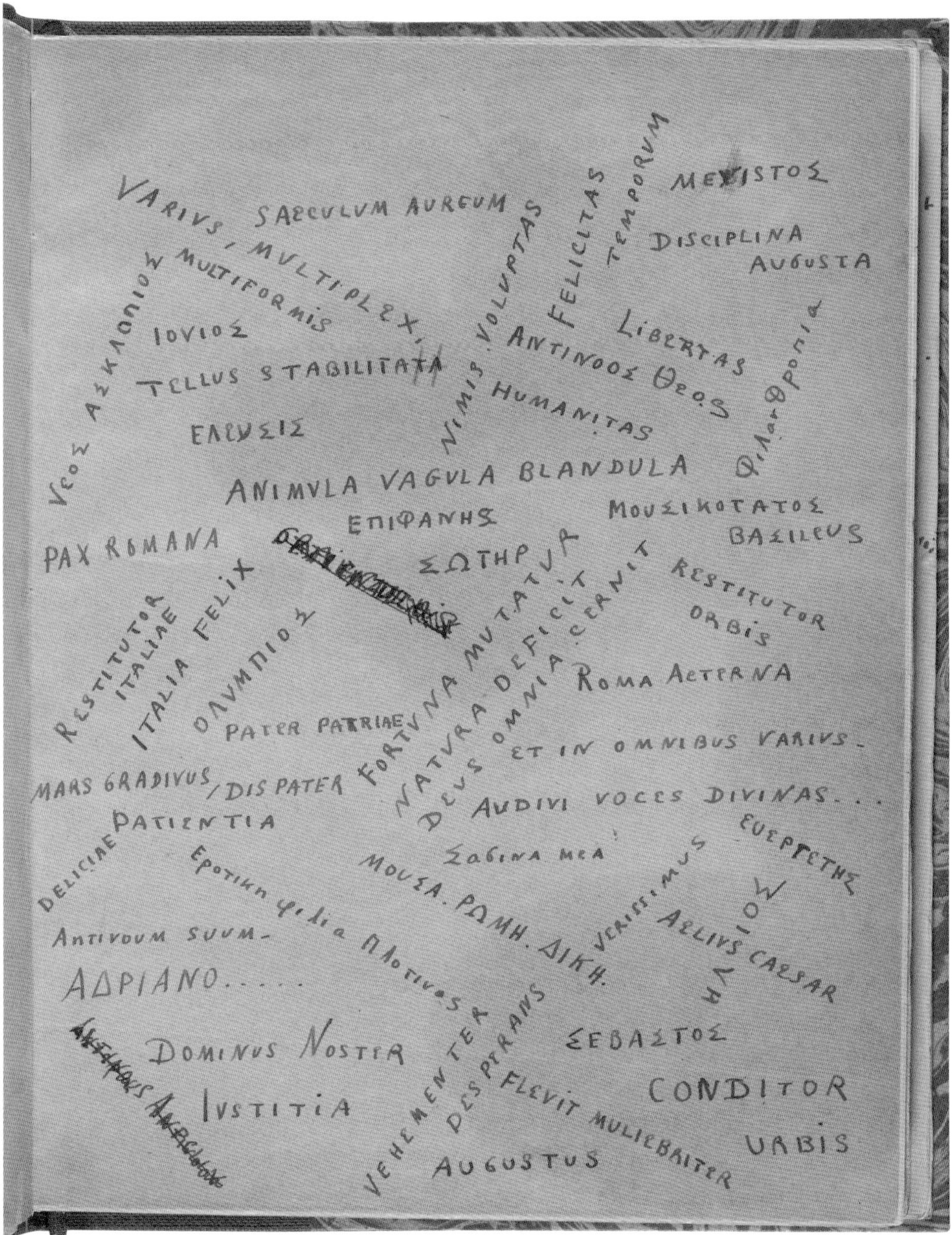

VARIVS, SAECVLVM AUREUM MEΓIΣTOΣ

MVLTIPLEX, TEMPORVM DISCIPLINA

MULTIFORMIS FELICITAS AUGUSTA

Νεος Ασκλεπιου IOVIOS NIMIS VOLUPTAS LIBERTAS Φιλανθρωπια

TELLUS STABILITATA ANTINOOS ΘεοS

ΕλΥΣΙΣ HUMANITAS

ANIMVLA VAGVLA BLANDULA

ΕΠΙΦΑΝΗΣ ΜΟΥΣΙΚΟΤΑΤΟΣ

PAX ROMANA ΣΩΤΗΡΙΑ ΒΑΣΙΛΕΥΣ

GRAECULUS RESTITUTOR

RESTITUTOR ITALIA FELIX ΟλΥΜΠΙΟΣ FORTVNA MUTATVR ORBIS

ITALIAE FELIX PATER PATRIAE NATVRA DEFICIT ROMA AETERNA

MARS GRADIVUS, / DIS PATER DEUS OMNIA CERNIT ET IN OMNIBUS VARIVS.

PATIENTIA AUDIVI VOCES DIVINAS...

DELICIAE Ερωτικη Φιλια Πλωτιναs Σαβινα mea MOUSA. ΡΩΜΗ. ΔΙΚΗ. ΕΥΕΡΓΕΤΗΣ

Antinoum suum— VERISSIMVS AΕΛΙΟΣ

ΑΔΡΙΑΝΟ..... AELIVS CAESAR

DOMINUS NOSTER VEHEMENTER ΣΕΒΑΣΤΟΣ CONDITOR

IVSTITIA DESPIRANS FLEVIT MULIEBRITER URBIS

AUGUSTUS

This etching shows a ruin, once thought to be dedicated to the memory of Antinous, in Hadrian's villa at Tivoli near Rome. A print of this still hangs over the fireplace in the living room of Yourcenar and Frick's house in Northeast Harbor, Maine.

Giovanni Battista Piranesi (1720–78), *Avanzi del Tempio del Dio Canopo nella Villa Adriana in Tivoli*. Rome, c. 1760–78.

Etching on paper, 45.5 x 58.5 cm.

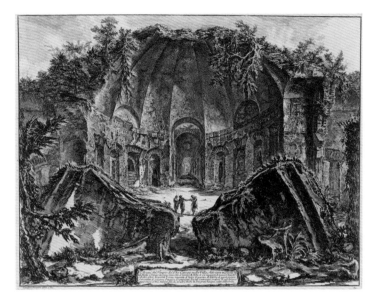

the ancient state monument with a small sign of the importance of the inner world of an individual, independent of all official history.

Yourcenar was the first woman ever to be elected to the French Academy in 1980. She defied any labels that could be attached to anyone's sexuality, and had left France to live with her partner and translator, Grace Frick (1903–79), in a small town on Mount Desert Island in Maine, USA. She did not dedicate *Memoirs of Hadrian* to anyone, but the notes to it carried a discreet virtual dedication to 'G. F...' as the ideal partner,

someone who is neither our shadow nor our reflection, nor even our complement but simply themselves; someone who leaves us ideally free, but who nevertheless obliges us to be fully what we are.

Frick's translation of the novel brought her partner greater international fame, but Frick's failing health delayed further translations of other books. Yourcenar, even at the height of her celebrity, refused to allow anyone else to translate her novels into English until after her partner's death. This determined gesture has been described by one French journalist, Bernard Pivot, as the most beautiful love story that he knew.

Yourcenar thought that history could and should be a 'school of liberty'. A brief look at the long history of same-sex desire across the world shows that it is an integral part of the human condition; it always has been part of humanity, and it always will be. History does not belong only to the 'mainstream' victors, and 'minorities' should not feel that they are marginal. On a long view, no one occupies the centre. It belongs to all of us.

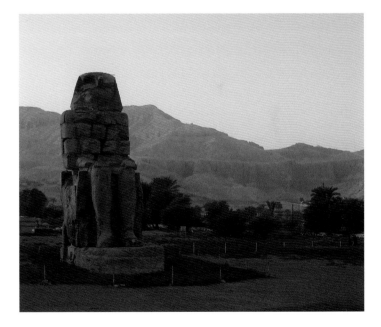

The scene of Hadrian's grief: the colossal statue of Pharaoh Amenhotep III from around 1375 BC that was a major tourist destination in ancient times. The official inscriptions recording the imperial visit are on the statue's left foot and ankle.

FURTHER RESOURCES

A version of this book is available as a web-trail:
britishmuseum.org/
samesexdesireandgenderidentity
(note that many of the objects are not on permanent
public display due to their fragility; this is particularly
the case with paper items).

For the objects in the British Museum see the
online collection database:
britishmuseum.org/research/search_the_
collection_database.aspx
Several objects that were once in the British
Museum's library are now in the British Library
(www.bl.uk).

This is only one museum collection and many
other resources are available. Some specialized
museums and collections exist, such as:

The Gay Museum in Berlin
(schwulesmuseum.de)

The lesbian, gay, bisexual and transgender
archive centre of IHLIA in Amsterdam
(ihlia.nl)

The GLBT History Museum in San Francisco
(glbthistory.org/museum/index.html)

Lesbian, gay, bisexual and transgender history
can be found everywhere and, for example, in
London there are significant holdings of world
and local histories at:

Untold London
(untoldlondon.org.uk)

The Museum of London
(museumoflondon.org.uk)

Victoria and Albert Museum
(vam.ac.uk/page/h/homosexuality)

The National Archives
(nationalarchives.gov.uk/records/research-
guides/gay-lesbian.htm)

London Metropolitan Archives
(lma.gov.uk)

The Hall-Carpenter Archives in the Library of the
London School of Economics and Political Science
(lse.ac.uk/library/archive/holdings/lesbian_
and_gay_archives.aspx)

Research on lesbian, gay, bisexual and transgender history progresses in many academic
institutions and is a specialist area in itself.
Many articles appear online, and monographs
can be found in specialized bookshops, such as
Gay's The Word in Bloomsbury
(freespace.virgin.net/gays.theword).

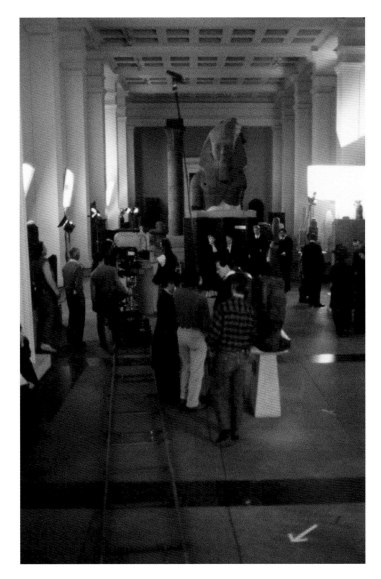

The museum as a stage for love:
Merchant Ivory Productions
filming E. M. Forster's *Maurice* in
the Egyptian sculpture gallery
in the British Museum, 1986.

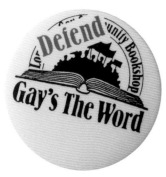

SUGGESTED GENERAL READING

R. Aldrich (ed.), *Gay Life and Culture: A World History.* London: Thames and Hudson 2006.

R. Aldrich, *Gay Life Stories.* London: Thames and Hudson 2012.

V. Baird, *The No-Nonsense Guide to Sexual Diversity.* Oxford: New Internationalist Publications 2007.

M. Cook et al., *A Gay History of Britain: Love and Sex between Men since the Middle Ages.* Oxford: Greenwood World Publishing 2007.

D. F. Greenberg, *The Construction of Homosexuality.* Chicago and London: University of Chicago Press 1988.

D. M. Halperin, *How to Do the History of Homosexuality.* Chicago and London: University of Chicago Press 2002.

S. Murray, *Homosexualities.* Chicago and London: University of Chicago Press 2000.

A. Sinfield, *Cultural Politics – Queer Reading.* Abingdon: Routledge 2005.

B. R. Smith, *Homosexual Desire in Shakespeare's England: A Cultural Poetics.* Chicago and London: University of Chicago Press 1994.

SOURCES FOR QUOTATIONS

p. 6 E. M. Forster (ed. P. Gardner), *Maurice*, 75. Abinger Edition 5; London: André Deutsch 1999.

p. 9 M. Yourcenar in M. Delcroix, *Marguerite Yourcenar, portrait d'une voix: Vingt-trois entretiens (1952–1987)*, 381 n. 1 (discussing the early twentieth century). Paris: Gallimard 2002.

p. 10 *The Tale of Horus and Seth*: P. UCL 32158 2.1; R. B. Parkinson, *Voices from Ancient Egypt: An Anthology of Middle Kingdom Writings*, 120. London: The British Museum Press 1991.

p. 11 E. M. Forster (ed. P. Gardner), *Maurice*, 183. Abinger Edition 5; London: André Deutsch 1999.

p. 14 'To Mrs M. A. at Parting': P. Loscocco (ed.), *Katherine Philips (1631/2–1664): Printed Poems 1667*, 76. *The Early Modern Englishwoman: A Facsimile Library of Essential Works Series II, Printed Works, 1641–1700*, Part 3, vol. 2; Aldershot: Ashgate 2007. Quote from Preface: [6].

p. 15 Quoted from B. Hinsch, *Passions of the Cut Sleeve*, 52–3. Berkeley, Los Angeles and Oxford: University of California Press 1990.

p. 17 Lister's Journals for 29 January 1821: H. Whitbread (ed.), *I Know My Own Heart: The Diaries of Anne Lister, 1791–1840*, 145. London: Virago 1988.

p. 17 'Heavy Date': W. H. Auden (ed. E. Mendelson), *Collected Poems*, 261. London: Faber and Faber 1991.

p. 19 B. R. Smith, *Homosexual Desire in Shakespeare's England: A Cultural Poetics*, 2. Chicago and London: University of Chicago Press 1994.

p. 19 Plato, *Charmides* (translated by D. Watt): T. J. Saunders et al., *Early Socratic Dialogues*, 178. Harmondsworth: Penguin 1987 [Author's italics in quote].

p. 20 Quoted from A. Sebba, *The Exiled Collector: William Bankes and the Making of an English Country House*, 177. London: John Murray 2004.

p. 20 Pers. comm. by B. Ewing about her novel *The Petticoat Men*. London: Head of Zeus 2014.

p. 22 H. Clinton speech on 6 December 2011: www.kaleidoscopetrust.com/features-letter-hilary-clinton.php.

pp. 23–4 A. Maupin, *Significant Others*, 123. London: Black Swan 1988.

p. 24 'Love, the Beloved Republic': E. M. Forster (ed. O. Stallybrass), *Two Cheers for Democracy*, 67 (citing A. Swinburne). Abinger Edition 11; London: Edward Arnold 1972.

p. 25 L. Kramer, *The Normal Heart*, 41 (Act II, scene 13). London: Methuen 1986.

p. 26 D. M. Halperin, *Saint Foucault: Towards a Gay Hagiography*, 62. New York and Oxford: Oxford University Press 1995.

p. 26 H. Fierstein, *Torch Song Trilogy*, 59 (*Widows and Children First!*, scene 1). London: Methuen 1984.

p. 27 D. Deitcher, *Dear Friends: American Photographs of Men Together, 1840–1918*, 150. New York: Harry N. Abrams 2001.

p. 29 E. M. Forster (ed. M. Lago and P. N. Furbank), *Selected Letters of E. M. Forster* I: *1879–1920*, 269. London: Collins 1983.

p. 37 *Erra and Ishum* Tablet IV: quoted from G. Leick, *Sex and Eroticism in Mesopotamian Literature*, 159, 168. London and New York: Routledge 1994.

p. 39 W. Holland, 'Mwah ... Is this the first recorded gay kiss?', *The Sunday Times*, 1 January 2006 (News, p. 3). Quote from stela 1. 18.

p. 40 *Gilgamesh* Tablet 1: S. Dalley, *Myths From Mesopotamia: Creation, The Flood, Gilgamesh and Others*, 58, 103. Oxford World's Classics; Oxford: Oxford University Press 2008.

pp. 42–3 Egyptian phrases: quoted from R. B. Parkinson, '"Homosexual" desire and Middle Kingdom literature', *Journal of Egyptian Archaeology* 81 (1995), 57–76.

p. 44 Sappho Fragments 16, 147: M. L. West, *Greek Lyric Poetry*, 37, 48. Oxford World's Classics; Oxford: Oxford University Press 1994.

p. 47 W. Hamilton, *Plato, The Symposium*, 42–3. Penguin Classics; Harmondsworth: Penguin 1951. © Walter Hamilton 1951.

p. 51 The 'Holy Grail': quoted from D. Williams, *The Warren Cup*, 26. Objects in Focus; London: The British Museum Press 2006.

p. 52 *The Dialogues of the Courtesans*, 5 Leaena and Clonarium: M. D. Macleod, *Lucian* VII, 379–81. Loeb Classical Library; London and Cambridge Massachusetts: William Heinemann and Harvard University Press 1961.

p. 54 *Historia Augusta*, Hadrian xiv: D. Magie, *The Scriptores Historiae Augustae* I, 44. Loeb Classical Library (3 vols); London and New York: William Heinemann and G. P. Putnam's Sons 1921 [translated by R. B. P.].

p. 55 A. Grimm and D. Kessler, *Der Obelisk des Antinoos: Eine kommentierte Edition*, 41. Munich: W. Fink 1994 [translated by R. B. P.].

p. 57 R. Vanita and S. Kidwai, *Same-sex Love in India: Readings from Literature and History*, xviii. New York: Palgrave 2001.

p. 60 *Inferno*, Canto 15 1. 106–8: C. S. Singleton, *Dante Alighieri, The Divine Comedy* (3 vols) I, 158. London:

Routledge and Kegan Paul 1971–5 [translated by R. B. P.].

p. 63 Quotes by Cortés and about Balboa from J. Goldberg, *Sodometries: Renaissance Texts, Modern Sexualities*, 193, 180. Stanford: Stanford University Press 1992.

p. 65 Poem no. 98: J. M. Saslow, *The Poetry of Michelangelo: An Annotated Translation*, 226. New Haven and London: Yale University Press 1991 [translated by R. B. P.].

p. 67 Quoted from G. M. Pflugfelder, *Cartographies of Desire: Male-Male Sexuality in Japanese Discourse 1600–1950*, 128. Berkeley, Los Angeles, London: University of California Press 2000.

p. 71 *As You Like It*, I.3, Sonnets 20 and 116: S. Wells and G. Taylor, *The Oxford Shakespeare: The Complete Works*, 661, 781, 793. Oxford: Clarendon Press 2005.

p. 73 Abu Nuwas, *Diwan* iv, 240: quoted from P. F. Kennedy, *Abu Nuwas: A Genius of Poetry*, 36. Makers of the Muslim World; Oxford: Oneworld 2005.

p. 73 Quoted from S. R. Canby, *Shah 'Abbas: The Remaking of Iran*, 251 (no. 123). London: The British Museum Press 2009.

p. 74 Broadsheet 1. 3, 26–9; translated by M. Marée.

p. 80 D. Samwell, *Some Accounts of a Voyage to South Sea's in 1776–1777–1778*, in J. C. Beaglehole (ed.), *The Voyage of the* Resolution *and* Discovery *1777–1780*, 1171–2. The Journals of Captain James Cook on his Voyages of Discovery 3, Part 2; Cambridge: Cambridge University Press for the Hakluyt Society 1967.

p. 82 Quotes from the 1841 Indictment and charge 'Queen v. Bankes', Dorset County Record Office.

p. 87 Quotes from D. Gaimster, 'Sex and Sensibility at the British Museum', *History Today* 50.9 (2000), 10–15.

p. 89 S. Vestal, *Warpath: the True Story of the Fighting Sioux Told in a Biography of Chief White Bull*, 265. Lincoln and London: University of Nebraska Press, 1962 [1934]. Quoted in

M. Carocci, 'Visualizing gender variability in Plains Indian pictographic art', *American Indian Culture and Research Journal* 33:1 (2009), 12.

p. 90 Visitor's comment: quoted from M. Cook, *London and The Culture of Homosexuality, 1885–1914*, 86 (a case study by R. von Krafft-Ebing). Cambridge Studies in Nineteenth-century Literature and Culture; Cambridge: Cambridge University Press 2003.

p. 90 *Maurice*: E. M. Forster (ed. P. Gardner), *Maurice*, 190. Abinger Edition 5; London: André Deutsch 1999.

p. 92 Archbishop Tutu: *The Lancet* 380 (2012), 428.

p. 95 Quoted from J. G. P. Delaney, *Charles Ricketts: A Biography*, 219. Oxford: Clarendon Press 1990.

p. 96 Letter by Augusta Kaiser of 31 December 1922: quoted from J. and A. Konietzny, *Augusta Kaiser – die Gustl Kaiser der Kieler Kunst-Keramik – und ihr Leben mit Hedwig Marquardt*, 14. Pansdorf: J. Konietzny 2011.

p. 99 V. Woolf (ed. R. Bowlby), *Orlando: A Biography*, 101–2. Oxford World's Classics; Oxford: Oxford University Press 1992.

p. 100 'Two Young Men, 23 to 24 Years Old': E. Sachperoglou, *C. P. Cavafy: The Collected Poems, A New Translation with Parallel Greek Text*, 168–71. Oxford World's Classics; Oxford: Oxford University Press 2007.

p. 104 Peter Tatchell: www.petertatchell.net.

p. 111 Artist's remarks: quoted from T. Hyman, *Bhupen Khakhar*, 68, 71. Bombay and Ahmedabad: Chemould Publications and Arts, and Mapin Publishing Pvt 1998. Remark by critic: 71.

p. 118–20 M. Yourcenar (translated by G. Frick), *Memoirs of Hadrian*, 174, 285. London: Penguin 1986. [Translation revised by R. B. P. to reflect the gender ambiguity of the original: the published English translation ('himself') is too discreet].

IMAGE CREDITS

p. 1 CM BNK,G.510 (given by the Bank of England)
p. 2 GR 2010,5006.611
p. 8 GR 1999,0426.1
p. 13 Photograph: R. B. Parkinson
p. 14 PD P,4.202
p. 17 Calderdale MBC Museums
p. 18 PD H,2.99
p. 21 PD 1868,0808.4299
p. 22 © Photo: Wei Quek, Photobolic
p. 27 © D. Deitcher
p. 28 © Merchant Ivory Productions; photograph by Jon Gardey
p. 29 Photograph: R. B. Parkinson
p. 32 CM 1991,1104.1; 1985,0625.5; 1985,0625.4
p. 35 PE 1958,1007.1
p. 36 ME 2003,0718.1
p. 38 EA 826
p. 39 Photograph: R. B. Parkinson
p. 40 ME 1853,0822.6
p. 41 ME K.913 (main part)
pp. 42–3 EA 10018.2
p. 44 P. Köln 21351+21376recto. Courtesy of the Papyrus Collection, Institut für Altertumskunde, University of Cologne
p. 45 CM BNK,G.510 (given by the Bank of England)
p. 46 GR 1865,1118.39 (given by Dr George Witt)
p. 47 GR 1843,1103.15
pp. 48–9 GR 1805,0703.227
pp. 50–1 GR 1999,0426.1
pp. 52–3 GR 2005,0921.1
p. 54 GR 1805,0703.95
p. 55 (left) Photograph by J. Williams, © The Trustees of the British Museum
p. 55 (right) GR 1805,0703.97
pp. 56–7 Asia 1987.0314.1 (Brooke Sewell Permanent Fund)
p. 58 (above and below left) PE 1925,1008.1 (given by Miss Lawrence)
p. 58 (below right) GR 1888,0301.1